Dean,

Welcome to the Vistage Chair Academy.

I look forward to greeting you when you arrive.

Genevieve

Praise for
The Power of Peers

"True peer advantage is an experience like no other. *The Power of Peers* shows you how to achieve it."

—Marshall Goldsmith, #1 *NY Times* best-selling
author of *Triggers, MOJO,* and *What Got You
Here Won't Get You There*

"There is no problem you can't solve if you have a group of peers watching your back. *The Power of Peers* makes a powerful case for peer groups and shows how to structure them, allowing any leader to accelerate an organization's scaling up."

—Verne Harnish, founder of Entrepreneurs' Organization
(EO) and author of *Scaling Up*

"Shapiro and Bottary know their stuff. Their combined experience plus the examples cited in this book make *The Power of Peers* a valuable walk-through into the world of what peer organizations can do to improve your leadership and success skills."

—Chris Brogan, CEO of Owner Media Group
and *NY Times* best-selling coauthor of *Trust Agents*

"*The Power of Peers* gives voice to a concept that I have long witnessed to be true in business – learning from others who have had similar or related experiences holds incredible value. Business owners are at a disadvantage if they do not have a set of people surrounding them to provide both counsel and support. From my own experience as a cofounder of a company, a journalist, and member of a peer group, I can say that peer advantage is the real deal."

—JJ Ramberg, host of MSNBC's *Your Business*
and cofounder of Goodshop

"In *The Power of Peers*, Shapiro and Bottary interview dozens of business leaders who tell a similar story to my own—that of seeking out a different kind of help from a group of peers—and in so doing provide a reasonable roadmap to help you learn what you just don't know."

—Gini Dietrich, CEO of Arment Dietrich
and author of *Spin Sucks*

"*The Power of Peers* provides a cogent and engaging explanation for *why* peer advisory groups work. So if you sit at the top of an organization or business and want to continually push your leadership and management performance to new levels, and do it in an environment that is supportive and fun, and yet hard-hitting and pragmatic, read this book."

—Craig Weber, author of *Conversational Capacity* and recipient of the Vistage Worldwide Speaker of the Year award

"Peer influence is evident in every stage of our life. Kids follow their friends and mirror their older siblings. Teenagers group together in cliques that walk, talk, and dress alike. As we mature, we grow as individuals, yet our peers remain a powerful force in our lives. We're all in this together. Whether it pertains to business or physical fitness, the more you surround yourself with peers who hold the same values and share the same goals, the more likely you are to accomplish those goals."

—Jesse Campanaro, CEO of Total Gym

"When I started my first business, most, if not all, decisions were mine. Ultimately, the business prospered, but if I had had a trusted peer group to share ideas with, I'm certain we would have been far more successful. With *The Power of Peers*, Leon Shapiro and Leo Bottary take you on a thoughtful journey that redefines the old adage of 'you are known (and far more successful) by the company you keep.' Read this book today and take action tomorrow, or you may look back years from now with just a bit of regret."

—Robert H. Thompson, author of *The Offsite: A Leadership Challenge Fable,* founder of LeaderInsideOut.com, and host of Robert Thompson's *Thought Grenades* radio

THE

POWER

OF

PEERS

THE
POWER
OF
PEERS

**How the Company You Keep Drives
Leadership, Growth & Success**

LEON SHAPIRO
AND LEO BOTTARY

First published by Bibliomotion, Inc.
39 Harvard Street
Brookline, MA 02445
Tel: 617-934-2427
www.bibliomotion.com

Printed in the United States of America

Library of Congress Cataloging-in-Publication Data

10   9   8   7   6   5   4   3   2

Names: Shapiro, Leon, 1958– author. | Bottary, Leo, author.
Title: The power of peers : how the company you keep drives leadership,
    growth, and success / Leon Shapiro and Leo Bottary.
Description: Brookline, MA : Bibliomotion, [2016] | Includes bibliographical
    references and index.
Identifiers: LCCN 2015049303 (print) | LCCN 2016001743 (ebook) | ISBN
    9781629561202 (hardback) | ISBN 9781629561219 (ebook) | ISBN 9781629561226
    (enhanced ebook)
Subjects: LCSH: Business networks. | Strategic planning. | Management. |
    Leadership. | BISAC: BUSINESS & ECONOMICS / Knowledge Capital. | BUSINESS
    & ECONOMICS / Leadership. | BUSINESS & ECONOMICS / Strategic Planning. |
    BUSINESS & ECONOMICS / Small Business.
Classification: LCC HD69.S8 S525 2016 (print) | LCC HD69.S8 (ebook) | DDC
    658/.046—dc23
LC record available at http://lccn.loc.gov/2015049303

To the family members, friends, colleagues,
and competitors who inspire us to be our best selves
and make the world a better place.

CONTENTS

PART III
Leading with Peer Advantage

FOREWORD

In the early 1990s, one of the most driven entrepreneurs of his generation hit a rough patch. Howard Schultz was trying to expand his Starbucks Coffee around the United States, but after opening a few hundred stores, his rapid expansion model began to break down. Reports came back that customer service, an ingredient perhaps even more important than the coffee itself, was dropping. Maybe the critics were right. It's darn near impossible to scale up a cult brand like Starbucks nationally, let alone worldwide. Why? The intangibles of a cult brand—that uniquely satisfying experience and great customer service—don't always respond to size and scale.

Schultz soon realized that what Starbucks needed most was someone with a deep appreciation for the art of customer satisfaction. Someone quite unlike Schultz, who was one of those type A, hypercompetitive, goal-oriented, numbers-driven, successful-at-everything-he-touches kind of guys.

So in 1994 Schultz did something unusual. He hired an outsider, his opposite in temperament, to strengthen employee morale and customer service at Starbucks. By the oddest of coincidences, the outsider also happened to be named Howard, Howard Behar.

"We were so unalike that it was funny," recalls Behar, who later rose to become president of Starbucks. "We look different. He's tall, athletic, hawkish. I'm short and round. We see the world differently, too. Hell, we argued and fought for three years about how important employee culture was to Starbucks's ability to delight the customer while scaling nationally and then worldwide. For Schultz, culture was maybe important, but not primary. For me, it was the whole game."

The Howard–Howard relationship had a rocky start. But the two protagonists stuck to it. Indeed, Howard Behar served as president of Starbucks for eight years under Howard Schultz.

How do I know this story of the two Howards? I learned about it while interviewing Howard Behar onstage at a Vistage Worldwide event in Seattle. Vistage is a peer-to-peer CEO organization whose members sign up precisely to get the kind of honest, often contrary advice that Howard Behar gave Howard Schultz.

The backstory of the Howard–Howard relationship at Starbucks is that Schultz, a dominant alpha male kind of CEO, was convinced that Starbucks's flat spot was a problem that could be teased out in spreadsheet analysis. The empathetic Behar thought otherwise. He told Schultz: "Give me three months to go talk to store managers and find out the real problem." While Schultz prowled the data looking for clues, Behar held conversations. At the end of three months Behar came back. During the next Starbucks board meeting, Behar stood up and gave his findings: "Board members, I just spent three months talking to store managers, and I'm afraid I have just one piece of data for you." The board members leaned forward to hear to Behar. "The store managers. They're unhappy. That's the sum of my data." Behar went on to explain that veteran store managers at Starbucks felt alienated from the company's growth. New managers didn't understand the Starbucks culture at all. Result: confusion and unhappiness. The foul mood translated to the baristas, whose bad attitude in turn alienated Starbucks customers.

Schultz and the board listened to Behar and agreed. Behar was tasked with fixing the Starbucks culture. The rest is history.

But what if Schultz and the board hadn't agreed with Behar? What if they'd found his statement "I'm afraid I have just one piece of data for you" a bit too cheeky? What if they had fired Behar instead of listening to him? Behar said he knew he was putting his job on the line by telling Schultz and the Starbucks board news they were not expecting. "I didn't care if they liked it or not," said Behar. "I knew it was the truth. I had run retail operations before."

The Howard–Howard story illustrates why CEO peer-to-peer groups are so valuable. Many CEOs of small and midsize companies do not regularly hear tough truths about their companies and their own performance as chief executives. Human nature being what it is, most CEOs have unwittingly set up their companies—and their boards of directors if they have them—to receive information that the employees and boards *think* the CEO wants to hear. Not what the CEOs should hear and need to hear.

To be a CEO of a small or midsize company is brutally hard. Lonely, too. Honest and empathetic advice is hard for CEOs to come by. Who does one talk to? Is it fair to burden the family? Dare one show doubt or vulnerability in front of employees, investors, or the board? Sure, one might confide difficulties to a therapist or coach, but what if the therapist or coach knows little about the specifics of the CEO's business?

Trusted CEO peer groups are the perfect answer to these solitary challenges and awesome responsibilities borne by men and women at the top. *The Power of Peers* by Leon Shapiro and Leo Bottary shows how to do this. It is the right book at the right time for CEOs today.

Rich Karlgaard
publisher and columnist
Forbes magazine

If you want to go fast . . . go alone.
If you want to go far . . . go together.
—African proverb

INTRODUCTION

You Don't Have to Go It Alone

The 1957 movie *Twelve Angry Men*, starring Henry Fonda, is among the most heralded feature films in history. Receiving three Oscar nominations, including Best Picture, the movie boasted an all-star supporting cast that included Lee J. Cobb, E. G. Marshall, Jack Warden, Ed Begley, and Jack Klugman, to name a few. These actors portrayed jurors who came from various walks of life and professional backgrounds, ranging from stockbroker, marketing executive, and architect to house painter, watchmaker, and inner-city hospital employee. They were not referred to by name in the film, only by their juror numbers.

As many of you may recall, the story revolves around this group of jurors working together to decide the fate of a boy who was accused of killing his father. After the judge delivered his instructions, they were sent to the jury room to begin deliberations. A guilty verdict would result in a mandatory sentence of the death penalty. A preliminary vote revealed that eleven of the twelve jurors believed the boy was guilty and, at the start of deliberations, those eleven jurors were convinced that all the talking in the world would not change their decision. Juror number eight, the lone holdout, wasn't sure whether the boy was guilty or not, but he thought that a boy's life was at least worth a conversation.

This confidential conversation among twelve anonymous jurors, which took place in the confines of one room, consumed ninety-three minutes of the ninety-six-minute film. No special effects. No elaborate action scenes. Yet you couldn't take your eyes off the screen. The stakes were life and death. The drama was palpable. The diversity of perspectives and the willingness of the jurors to dig deep and ask the hard questions revealed that much of the evidence was unreliable and it was unlikely the boy could have committed the murder. One by one, with what began as an eleven-to-one guilty vote, the jurors changed their minds, resulting in a unanimous verdict for the boy's acquittal. The collective wisdom of the group prevailed.

Coincidentally, in the same year the film was released, Bob Nourse assembled a group of CEOs in Milwaukee, Wisconsin, and called it The Executive Committee, more commonly referred to as TEC. Bob's vision was clear: *If you bring together CEOs with diverse experiences from noncompeting industries who share the dream of growing healthy, vibrant companies, there isn't any problem they can't solve or any goal they won't achieve—as long as they work together.* By collaborating in a confidential setting, these CEOs would help one another make better decisions. Here, the stakes are high as well. The lives of company employees, their families, and their communities depend upon the decisions and good judgment of the executives who fuel the engine that drives the world economy. Being a CEO or small business owner is not a responsibility anyone needs to bear alone.

In *Twelve Angry Men,* the jury reached a wise decision because the members listened to one another's perspectives (shaped by their diverse backgrounds and experiences) and were relentless in their examination of the evidence. Despite conflicting personalities and some very intense moments, they were eventually united by their pursuit of the truth. As the deliberations so clearly illustrated, not a single member of the jury, not even juror number eight, would have ever come to such a certain conclusion by himself. As a group, they uncovered the truth and reached the right decision.

THE VALUE OF BEING IN A CEO GROUP

Leon shares a story that captures the value he discovered after joining a CEO Peer Advisory Group:

When I joined Vistage as CEO in April 2013, I was both excited about the opportunity and confident that my experience had prepared me well for the role. I had spent most of my career working in membership organizations and leveraging the power of peers as a learning and collaboration tool. I was assuming the leadership of a fifty-five-year-old business where I would be surrounded by hundreds of ex-CEOs (Vistage Group chairs/facilitators), an experienced board of directors, and a culture that espoused helping CEOs become better and more effective leaders. With so many advisors and so many resources available to me, I thought, "What could go wrong?"

On Thanksgiving night of that first year, I woke at two a.m. and could not fall back asleep. I assumed it was a "turkey hangover" and decided to get up and do some work on a strategy presentation for our upcoming board meeting. I had been struggling with conflicting strategies and choices for weeks, and while I had received lots of feedback from my discussions with my leadership team, my board, and key stakeholders in the community, it was time to make some tough decisions.

I sat and stared at my laptop for hours, getting nowhere fast. I was inundated with advice and counsel from very talented, experienced, supportive, and caring people. I had many advisors who wanted to help me. However, there's a reason the expression "It's lonely at the top" is used so frequently.

All of the advice and counsel I was getting, while well intentioned, was largely subjective. Board members would listen and offer input, but too often they didn't have enough information, or they were guided by investor requirements. My management team, wanting to be supportive, had a natural propensity to tell me what they believed I wanted to hear or to protect the interest of their function and staff. My friends and family were supportive but not always willing to tell me the whole truth. Paid advisors and consultants had a narrow view based on their particular expertise and were also motivated to maintain their relationship with me for as long as possible. There was nowhere for me to turn that would allow me to be myself, authentic and transparent, let alone share the perspective of what it was like to walk in the CEO's shoes.

The truth is that after joining Vistage as CEO, I initially resisted joining a CEO peer advisory group. I believed at the time that, as a new CEO, I brought a fresh perspective to the business that would benefit the organization in ways existing employees could not. I did not want to become an "insider" too quickly. Moreover, I felt that the depth of my experience around peer learning meant that I understood the value proposition as well as anyone.

It wasn't until I actually joined a Vistage group that I found the objectivity, diversity of experience, and perspective I needed. My group was willing to tell me the hard truth without sugarcoating it. My fellow members would unabashedly question my assumptions and ask, "Why not?" if they thought I was dismissing obvious solutions or succumbing to self-limiting beliefs. They offered a sounding board, listening to all of my ideas without judgment. They found a way to help me refine my thinking and gave me the confidence I needed to act on those decisions with conviction.

The other CEOs in my group held me accountable to any and all commitments I had made. I finally had a trusted and safe space where I could be truly transparent and share without fear of judgment. Until I experienced being in a group, I had no idea what I was missing.

CEOS STRUGGLE WITH ISOLATION

According to a study conducted at Stanford Graduate School of Business, nearly two-thirds of CEOs do not receive outside leadership advice.[1] These CEOs struggle with isolation and a sense that they are lonely at the top. The implications of this isolation can be detrimental to a CEO's effectiveness, particularly in the fast-changing, increasingly complex world in which we live.

Those CEOs who seek outside help to address their feelings of isolation typically read leadership books, hire executive coaches, retain consulting companies, attend industry conferences, and/or enroll in CEO executive development programs offered at business schools across the country—none of which addresses the problem at its core. The solution to CEO isolation can't be found in a book, learned in a course, or gleaned from a coach alone.

The answer lies in working with a group of CEOs from diverse industries who can empathize with the complexities of the position, provide different perspectives to shared challenges and opportunities, and create a culture of collegiality and accountability that eliminates the isolation and inspires improved personal and organizational performance. By working with their peers in a manner that's highly selective, strategic, and structured, CEOs can transform garden-variety peer influence into something much more powerful—something we call *peer advantage*.

LEO'S INTEREST IN CEO PEER ADVISORY GROUPS

The prospect of writing this book with Leon inspired me to reflect on my own journey and consider what events moved me to become so fascinated by our peers and peer advisory groups. My first professional peer group experience began when I joined the Worldcom Public Relations Group—a consortium of more than 100 of the best-in-market independent PR agencies in the world. In the mid-1990s, I founded Bottary & Partners Public Relations, which was headquartered in Jacksonville, Florida. Because my firm would frequently compete with other PR agencies that had multinational offices, I applied and was accepted as a Worldcom PR Group member. I saw it as a way to give me a set of trusted, best-in-class independent agencies with which I could affiliate and extend my firm's reach and capabilities. While being a member achieved the intended marketing objectives for the firm, I was most impressed by what I learned from the other agency principals. The meetings afforded me the opportunity not only to exchange ideas and best practices with other agency leaders, but also to build trust—a crucial element when it came to sharing client work.

Later, as both a student and an instructor, I actively participated and played leadership roles on learning teams at Seton Hall University, Pepperdine, and Northeastern. Because these teams are comprised of mid-to-senior level executives and educators, the participants tend to learn as much or more from one another as they do from the academic material or the instructor. The experience at Worldcom Public Relations Group and in higher education piqued my interest in joining Vistage when a position became available in early 2010. I was particularly intrigued by how CEOs would be helped by fellow members who are in completely different industries from their own. I spent a great deal of time attending Vistage Group meetings around the country and soon learned that these CEOs had far more in common than not, and what they didn't have in common only served as learning opportunities for sharing industry best practices that could be applied anywhere. By stepping outside of their companies and industry silos, they deepened their knowledge and expanded their worldview. I eventually joined a Vistage Key Executive Group and a Vistage Inside Group (a group of VP level Vistage executives who focus on collaboration and professional development). All of this led to my pursuing an Ed.D. in Organizational Leadership, with a focus on how peer advisory groups deliver learning value to CEOs.

WHY WE WROTE THIS BOOK

Quite simply, we want to introduce more leaders to the power of peers. While thousands of CEOs and business owners will tell you that being part of a CEO peer advisory group has transformed their lives and their companies, too many others don't avail themselves of this resource. By giving new language to what CEO peer advisory groups are all about, we hope more CEOs and business owners will discover how much they (and their organizations) can benefit.

When we first considered the idea of writing a book, we joked about the episode from Seinfeld where Kramer unveils the coffee table book about coffee tables. If you recall, Kramer showed us how the book itself doubled as—you guessed it—a coffee table. Although we work for a company that's in the business of assembling and facilitating peer advisory groups here in the US and around the world, the last thing we wanted to do was write the Vistage book about Vistage. The Vistage Board and Executive Leadership Team agreed. Our charge here is much bigger than that.

To describe all the currencies that comprise the value we receive from our peers, we examined a great deal of research and reached out to colleagues and competitors alike so they could share their insights and stories for this book. While some of the names and companies portrayed have been changed to respect confidentiality, all the stories are true. These interviews were invaluable to helping us paint a more complete picture of what peer advantage is all about. Our job was simply to ask the right questions.

Without giving it a second thought or that much effort, we experience the power of peer influence every day. It's been that way our whole lives. Imagine if we gave it a second thought. Consider what would happen if we were more purposeful about how we harnessed that power. The truth is, we can help each other in ways we can't find anywhere else. If you want to grow as an individual, become a better leader, and prepare your organization to meet the challenges of the future, simply step up your level of engagement with a group of peers you respect and who are committed to the same goals, and watch what happens!

There are very few books, at least in the business and education arena, dedicated to those who stand beside us. We thought our peers and the value we glean from those relationships deserved a closer look.

HOW THIS BOOK IS ORGANIZED

The book is divided into three distinct parts. Part 1, "Peer Influence in a Complex World," examines why peer influence matters for CEOs and business leaders. It begins by tapping into a principle you intuitively understand and have experienced: who you surround yourself with matters. It explores the pervasive power of peer influence and how, for as long as you can remember, you've experienced it each and every day—sometimes in obvious ways and other times without even noticing. We focus the conversation by examining the four most common ways we engage our peers, recommending a new set of peer engagement priorities specifically for CEOs and business owners, and introduce the five factors that make peer advantage possible.

Peer advantage is not an individual pursuit; it's a group endeavor. Part 2, "The Five Factors for Peer Advantage," identifies the essentials for any CEO peer advisory group that wishes to enjoy the fruits of peer advantage. If you're already convinced as you read this introduction that peer influence is something you'd like to harness and leverage to greater advantage, feel free to start with part 2. (You can always go back to part 1 later.)

Part 3, "Leading with Peer Advantage," suggests that organizational and business growth begins with you. You'll read how other CEOs have grown individually and how peer advantage has changed their lives. You'll see that stepping outside your company and industry, and working with a diverse group of your peers, will give you a better vantage point for meeting challenges and identifying future opportunities.

Surround yourself with the right people and employ the five factors for realizing peer advantage, and there isn't a challenge too big to meet or an aspiration too lofty to achieve. Let's get started!

PART I

Peer Influence in a Complex World

1

Are You a Peerless Leader?

CEOs are faced with a singular reality: there are very few people they can rely upon for impartial advice. It's just not that easy to find individuals who know precisely what it's like to sit in the CEO's chair. We'll introduce you to CEOs—from a range of industries and from companies of various sizes—who have turned to their peers to help them become better leaders and build stronger companies. Meet Paul Caskey.

In 1983, a year after receiving his bachelor of science degree in chemical engineering, Paul Caskey joined CCP, Inc., a contract manufacturer of hair bleaching powders for the cosmetic industry. Located in northern New Jersey, the company had just $640,000 in sales, employed ten people, and had never turned a profit. Paul was named general manager and reported directly to owners who were not active in the business.

Within a few short years, Paul grew the company to $4 million in sales and was named CEO. With more than 90 percent of its revenues derived from hair bleach products, the company continued at a pace of slow, steady growth. Having begun at CCP pretty much right out of school, Paul realized that, as leader of a growing company, he would soon test the limits of his knowledge and experience. Paul understood that—with absentee owners, a lack of exposure to industries outside his own, and no one in the organization who knew what it was like to sit in the CEO's chair—he needed help.

LONELY AT THE TOP

Paul's situation was not unlike that of many CEOs, whether they are new to the position or have served as a CEO in the past. As we touched on in the introduction, a study conducted by the Center for Leadership Development and Research (CLDR) at Stanford Graduate School of Business, Stanford University's Rock Center for Corporate Governance, and The Miles Group revealed that many CEOs struggle with isolation and a sense that they are "lonely at the top."[1] Nearly two-thirds of CEOs do not receive outside leadership advice, while 100 percent of respondents stated that they would be open to making changes based on feedback. Stephen Miles, CEO of The Miles Group, stated, "Even the best-of-the-best CEOs have their blind spots and can dramatically improve their performance with an outside perspective weighing in."

The idea that being a CEO is a solitary pursuit is a misapprehension. Author and founder of Virgin Group Richard Branson once said, "Many people think that an entrepreneur is someone who operates alone, overcoming challenges and bringing his idea to market through sheer force of personality. This is completely inaccurate. Few entrepreneurs—scratch that: almost no one—ever achieved anything worthwhile without help."[2]

To address the feeling of isolation that can be so limiting and constraining for anyone leading an organization, CEOs typically draw from a broad range of resources including coaches, consulting companies, industry events, and executive education. These are all worthwhile and effective pursuits, and according to CEOs we interviewed from myriad organizations of varying sizes, they are among the most popular ways CEOs learn, grow, and address being *lonely at the top*. Paul tried something different.

HOW CEOS TEACH ONE ANOTHER

Paul filled the gaps he believed could limit his ability to successfully lead CCP, Inc., into the future by joining a local CEO advisory group. The group was made up of a dozen of his peers from various industries.

Initially, Paul questioned how such a diverse group could help meet his unique needs, thinking, "How will CEOs who know nothing about my specific business or my industry help me?" Also, given the size of the group, he wondered, "How much time are we really going to spend on issues that impact my company?"

Similar to Team In Training, a sports training program in which people who want to complete a marathon or other endurance event surround themselves with others who share the same goal, a typical CEO advisory peer group is made up of high-performing CEOs who want to grow as leaders and build thriving organizations. By coming together, CEOs help one another realize their respective individual goals. Rather than learning by reading case studies, they work in real time on actual business issues. Being part of a group provides each CEO a broader range of perspectives than she would likely receive from the people at her company.

CEO peer groups also provide another important benefit. Once CEOs become exposed to the value that comes from engaging with their own peers, they begin to see their organization horizontally as well as vertically. They pay more attention to the power of peers in their organizational structure and start to tap into the key influencers more frequently. This peer power, when channeled properly, serves as a wellspring for driving organizational excellence.

SOLVING A SEASONALITY PROBLEM

Paul's CEO advisory group meetings typically started with a check-in, during which group members offered brief updates on what was happening in their lives personally and professionally. One August morning, when it was Paul's turn to talk about what was going on at his company, he briefly shared a situation that he dealt with each year during the summer months. Paul explained that when it comes to manufacturing hair bleaching powders, the amount of moisture in the air matters. A lot. Think of the chemistry of hair bleaching powders as similar to that of solid rocket propellant—the substance can react violently with moisture. Therefore, it was too dangerous to manufacture the bleaching powders during the humid summer months, and Paul's company had to cease production. This resulted in a 25 percent underutilization of the company's facility during that period.

When Paul finished offering his overview, he assumed the next person would take her turn. Instead, one of the members asked, "Why is that acceptable? Isn't there anything else you could be doing instead?" Having grown up in the hair bleach business, Paul had never considered alternatives that could resolve the issue of seasonality.

When Paul returned to his company, he asked himself why the situation was acceptable and began to explore his options. First, he and his team identified items that could be produced using equipment the company already had in place. Knowing that it is easier to gain additional business from existing customers than to attract new ones, he focused on items that his current customer base would need. Soon after, CCP embarked on a line of bath salts, fragranced talcum powders, and drawer sachets, all of which could be manufactured with no modifications to existing equipment and would be purchased by CCP's existing customer base. While these products are produced year round, their production tends to be heavily weighted in the summer months to gear up for the Christmas/Hanukkah holiday season. Furthermore, these products were not hazardous and they carried higher profit margins because the formulas were developed at CCP.

Within a year, CCP added $4 million in sales at higher profit margins, which doubled the business, dramatically increased profitability, and removed the seasonality problem. Within five years, CCP grew to $12.5 million in sales, with 120 employees producing numerous items for the hair, bath, and body markets, and Paul eventually moved on.

Paul suggested that the real value from this peer advisory experience didn't come from peers answering his questions; rather, it came from CEOs questioning his answers. As Paul reflected on his group experience, he noted several other major benefits he would not have received anywhere else:

■ **Impartiality**—Employees and board members, regardless of their espoused objectivity and true sincerity, have a personal stake in the outcome of business decisions. Fellow CEOs are not burdened with that extra layer of consideration—they have no agenda other than to help one another. They can ask the hard questions and challenge assumptions without regard for sacred cows, personal relationships, or other organizational/industry blinders. It's an eye-opening experience for many CEOs when peers look at a specific challenge through a completely impartial lens.

■ **Shared challenges**—While the CEOs in peer groups may serve entirely different types of customers in widely varying industries, they share common challenges regarding employees, growth, profitability, executive development, technology, and uncertainty, to name just a few. In fact, their diversity enhances the group's learning by the breadth and depth of their background and experience. The more they talk, the more they realize how much they have in common and how much they can learn from one another.

■ **Learning**—While they share challenges, the myriad industries they represent, the size of the organizations they lead, and the depth of their experience set the table for rich conversations about proven practices for effective leadership. Sharing ideas across industries, differing stages of growth, and changing business challenges enriches the learning experience. By helping one another through this process, these CEOs will also share their personal triumphs and failures. This display of trust creates an environment in which the CEO can be truly vulnerable, open to learning and growing. And unlike one-to-one executive coaching, which can be a rich complement to the peer advisory experience, peer advisory groups harness the unique power of the group dynamic.

■ **Empathy**—If you've never been a CEO, it's nearly impossible to put yourself in a CEO's shoes. It's difficult for most of us, regardless of how much we care or how objective we believe we are in offering counsel to our CEOs, to imagine what that's really like. Fellow CEOs are looking at the whole picture because that's what they do every day— they can identify with their fellow CEOs. The empathy that one CEO shares with another is felt not only professionally but personally as well.

■ **Owning the solution**—Unlike consulting firms, which offer recommendations, peer advisory groups help individual members come to their own conclusions about the actions they are prepared to take to achieve a particular goal. The dynamic of owning your own solution versus implementing a recommendation that's been imposed on you can make all the difference in the world when it comes to effective execution.

Paul recalled that when he started at CCP there were only ten employees. During his tenure, the number of employees grew to 120. Paul credits the peer-to-peer experience he gained in his CEO group with enlightening him to the power of peers and the way it factors into building a winning team. Not surprisingly, Paul credits his people for the role they played in driving organizational excellence at CCP.

COMMUNITIES OF PRACTICE

In 1991, Etienne Wenger-Trayner and Jean Lave coined the term *communities of practice*,[3] which was described a decade later as "Groups of people who share a concern, a set of problems, or a passion about a topic, and who deepen their knowledge and expertise in this area by interacting on an ongoing basis."[4] The structural characteristics of a community of practice include having a domain that involves a common knowledge base around a shared purpose, a community willing to collaborate, and a practice with a shared set of approaches, language, and tools. All of these elements are present in a CEO peer advisory group.

Those who lead these CEO communities of practice do so by:

- Using open-ended questions to promote active problem solving
- Creating social interdependence and setting clear goals through collaboration
- Creating an environment of trust, confidentiality, and transparency
- Utilizing tools that help participants organize their knowledge
- Playing the role of facilitator rather than coach

When we talked to Etienne and Beverly Wenger-Trayner, who today are active researchers, consultants, and authorities on the topic, they explained that communities of practice have been around since the dawn of human existence, but once they had a name and a common language, it became easier to talk about them and cultivate them intentionally.

While studying historical cases of apprenticeship with anthropologist Jean Lave, Etienne recalled, "Initially, we were studying apprenticeship as a way to rethink learning. We found that an apprenticeship is often not just a relationship between a master and a student. We noticed this whole community around the master that acts as a learning curriculum for the apprentice. A lot of the learning interactions were not with the master, they were with one another. This is essentially where the term communities of practice comes from."

In an article cowritten by Etienne and William Snyder for *Harvard Business Review* in 2000, they noted that communities of practice were common in classical Greece, where "corporations" of craftsmen had both a social purpose and a business function.[5] The members trained one another and worked together to share innovations. During the Middle Ages, guilds offered a similar resource for artisans.

MASTERMIND GROUPS

In early American history, Benjamin Franklin organized a group of twelve friends called the Junto to provide an ongoing forum for structured discussion.[6] The group's original members included printers, surveyors, a cabinetmaker, a cobbler, a clerk, and a merchant. They met on Friday evenings to talk about morals, politics, and natural philosophy. Franklin stated, "Our debates were to be under the direction of a president, and to be conducted in the sincere spirit of inquiry after truth, without fondness for dispute or desire of victory."

In 1743, the Junto would become the American Philosophical Society, created "to promote useful knowledge in the colonies" and still active to this day.[7]

In business, Napoleon Hill's book *Think and Grow Rich* described the advent of the mastermind group and how both Andrew Carnegie and Henry Ford credited their mastermind groups for much of their success. Hill regarded these groups as the secret to the success of all great men and foundational to all outstanding personal achievements. A mastermind group called the Vagabonds included Henry Ford, Thomas Edison, President Warren G. Harding, and Harvey Firestone—a pretty formidable collection of peers![8]

MILLENNIALS SEEK CONNECTIONS

While it may be fascinating to imagine being in a peer group with Henry Ford and Thomas Edison, or the interesting conversations Ben Franklin must have led during Junto meetings, the richer conversation may lie in the role peer advisory groups will play in the future. This is particularly important because, as of 2015, millennials represented 45 percent of employees in the workforce—and 28 percent of them served in management roles.[9]

While 82 percent of hiring managers regard the millennial generation as more technically adept than previous ones, this generation is also characterized as caring a great deal about their work colleagues.[10] They may have grown up in a digital world, but they are hungry for in-person experiences as well. And because many of these employees have experienced group work as part of their educational experience, their inclination to collaborate rather than compete is already translating into the workplace. Best-selling author and business advisor Chris Brogan added, "There is a big appetite for face-to-face meetings, particularly when it comes to closing a deal. I'm also seeing a trend toward young people engaging more deeply with smaller affinity groups as opposed to using social media as a means to amass a high number of followers."

Bob Berk leads a group of high-potential millennials, from a range of small to midsized companies, who participate in quarterly leadership development sessions with their peers in the Chicago area. Their full-day and half-day face-to-face sessions give them a chance to build trust and dig deeper than they would have the opportunity to do online. They can't get enough face-to-face interaction.

In communities of practice, both past and present, learning is what happens in practice. "The essence of a community of practice is that you don't detach the practice from the practitioner," Etienne Wenger-Trayner said. "You don't detach knowledge from the knower. You don't detach learning from the learner. Becoming a good CEO is not just acquiring knowledge and skills; it's embodying these as a way of being a certain kind of person. It includes who you are. You cannot detach who you are from an understanding of the practice. I think that's where a community can become really transformative." CEO peer advisory groups don't study and analyze case histories from other organizations; they work on their current issues and challenges in real time, so that those challenges of practice drive a shared learning agenda, with the ongoing learning from that agenda being fed right back into the practice of what is happening in their own companies. It is an iterative cycle of practice informing a learning agenda, which informs practice.

THE PATH FROM PEER INFLUENCE TO PEER ADVANTAGE

Often, business leaders enlist peer engagement in varying degrees outside of peer advisory groups. Understanding the ways we engage our peers can help us discern the difference between the peer influence we experience every day and the *peer advantage* that can result from a more strategic and structured approach. In essence, we work with our peers in four distinct ways: we connect, network, optimize, and accelerate.

We **connect** with our peers in person or online. The people we connect with are typically acquaintances—though they may be people we've never met—with whom we exchange information or share a common interest, even if only temporarily. Think in terms of attending general business gatherings in your local community, seeking opinions about vendor experiences on Yelp, or connecting at the most basic levels on LinkedIn.

We **network** online, at conferences, or at local business events and socials in a more selective and more purposeful attempt to advance personal and professional interests. Connecting and networking tend to be individual pursuits and are, by far, the most common ways we reach out to our peers.

There's a difference between the peer influence most organizational leaders experience when they connect and network, and the peer advantage that can be realized when leaders work with others to optimize and accelerate. This is among the fundamental principles of this book. We **optimize** when we work together in teams to bring a high level of excellence to achieving a common goal. Leaders often form organizational "tiger teams" to tackle special projects. The Blue Angels, the U.S. Navy's flight demonstration squadron, conducts debriefs following every (what we see as perfect) flight to talk about how they can do better the next time. Top sports teams participate in practices that are often more rigorous than the games to ensure top performance when it truly counts. The work of optimizing tends to take place among a more homogenous group of peers and be temporary in nature, determined by either the length of a specific project or the span of a season.

We define **accelerate** as the ultimate means for gaining peer advantage. It's what top CEOs do when they work together as part of a diverse group on an ongoing basis. The objectives are to help one another meet tough challenges, achieve lofty organizational goals, and grow as leaders. Examples of groups that serve CEOs in this manner are CCI, Entrepreneurs' Organization (EO), True North Group, Vistage, and Young Presidents' Organization (YPO), among others. Other groups that employ the accelerate concept are those led by the Milken Institute and the World Economic Forum. These groups bring together highly influential people from various walks of life to address many of society's most complex challenges.

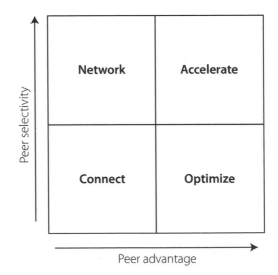

FIGURE 1.1   Peer Engagement Framework

PEER ADVANTAGE IS PEER INFLUENCE OF A HIGHER ORDER

Whether you want to double the size of your company or build an exit strategy, being around a select group of people who share your commitment to success is a transformative experience. Peer advisory groups that optimize and accelerate business growth employ five factors that are essential to the group experience and to achieving desired outcomes. We'll spend part 2 of the book describing these factors in great detail because they are so essential to a group's success:

1. Select the right peers—find true peers who share your commitment to excellence.
2. Create a safe environment—cultivate an atmosphere that is judgment-free, inspiring open dialogue and deep learning.
3. Utilize a smart guide—someone who can effectively facilitate the conversation.
4. Foster valuable interaction—establish a process that encourages rich and meaningful conversation.
5. Be accountable—honor a shared expectation that you will do what you say you will do.

Later in the book, we will address the following questions:

- What does it take to harness peer advantage?
- How can peer advantage inspire individual growth?
- How can peer advantage help you solve complex challenges and lead in a world of uncertainty?

SUMMARY

No CEO, business owner, or organizational leader should ever have to go it alone. While there are myriad resources available for CEOs who want to learn and grow, there's no better way to combat the feeling of being lonely at the top than being part of a CEO group. Learning in communities is as natural to humans as breathing, and being part of a community that shares a domain, a willingness to collaborate, and a common purpose can be a truly transformative experience. Next, let's consider how the pervasive nature of peer influence permeates our lives and provides a platform for taking your business and your life to new heights.

2

The Pervasive Nature of Peer Influence

In 1986, Bruce Cleland and his wife, Izzi, learned that their two-year-old daughter, Georgia, had leukemia and that the survival rate was only 55 percent.[1] Like any parents, they were devastated by the news. As they immersed themselves in the world of blood cancer treatments, they learned a great deal about the disease and became deeply involved with the work of the Leukemia & Lymphoma Society (LLS). After two years of treatments, Georgia's cancer was in remission.

Cleland had an idea that would both honor his daughter and express his appreciation to the many people at the Leukemia & Lymphoma Society who helped his family through that difficult time. Rather than host a traditional fundraiser, he decided to raise money by running his first marathon. He reached out to friends at LLS and eventually assembled a total of thirty-eight people to run the New York City Marathon.

While Cleland obtained a few corporate sponsors, it was the group members themselves who raised a significant portion of the money by asking friends and coworkers to pledge a specific dollar amount per mile for each of the twenty-six miles, assuming they completed the race. With the help of his friend Rod Dixon (who won the race in 1983) and Jeff Galloway's marathon training program, the group made a commitment to one another to train for and complete the marathon.

During the four to five months before the race, the group met regularly at a local restaurant or bar, where they compared notes and discussed their progress. Cleland recalls being impressed with everyone's commitment to training and completing the race. After a great deal of hard work, the mutual support paid off for everyone involved. All thirty-eight runners crossed the finish line, raising a staggering $322,000 for blood cancer research. Those runners who completed the New York City Marathon that day did it by working together. They shared a passion for the goal and the cause, which was strengthened by working together as a group and having one another to lean on for encouragement and support.

For Bruce Cleland, running the New York City Marathon and raising $322,000 for the Leukemia & Lymphoma Society was just the beginning. From the start, Bruce insisted that the thirty-eight runners were a team—the team that just happened to kick off what is now the most successful endurance-sport fundraising program in the world. To date, Team In Training has inspired more than 650,000 participants to achieve their personal goals and raise $1.3 billion for blood cancer research. Best of all, the rate of survival for blood cancer, which was 55 percent in the 1980s, is 95 percent today.[2]

This story illustrates the power of the group dynamic and how your peers can help you achieve your personal best and positively impact the lives of others in the process. It is a fitting illustration of the phrase "Together, anything is possible."

Peer influence is such a significant part of our personal development that it has become embedded in the English language: Birds of a feather flock together. We're all in the same boat. Great minds think alike. You're known by the company you keep. While just figures of speech to some, these statements reflect the simple truth that our peers matter. Phrases like these underscore a basic assumption: surround yourself with the wrong people and they will drag you down. Build relationships with the right people—those who share your aspirations and the commitment to achieve them—and they will lift you to heights you never dreamed possible.

IT STARTS WHEN WE'RE YOUNG

Our parents understood the power of peer influence. They realized that even in an ideal parent-child relationship, peers wield enormous power.

It's why they were always so inquisitive about our friends and classmates. When we made new friends, our parents would see the effects of these relationships in our behavior—from the words we chose to the way we acted at home or at school. Peer influence starts early and affects our children's lives at all grade levels.

In Gary Ladd's 2005 book, *Children's Peer Relations and Social Competence: A Century of Progress,* he examines the role of peer relationships in child and adolescent development, having tracked major research findings in the field since the 1900s. Ladd is a professor of psychology and human development at Arizona State University. He says that the types of peer relationships children form differ from those they have with parents and siblings and, as a result, teach them unique skills that impact their development. Peer relationships are more balanced, and children tend to bring similar levels of ability and reasoning to their interactions.[3]

When Leon's oldest child, Danielle, boarded the school bus for her first day of high school, he turned to his wife Debra and said: "Our ability to influence and shape Danielle's thinking is going to evaporate in front of our eyes." They knew that for the next four years Danielle's development and her worldview would be influenced primarily by her high school friends. The decisions she would make regarding her social circles, choice of college, and career path would all be swayed by her peers.

Leon and Debra determined that getting to know her friends would be their top priority. They decided they would open up their home to Danielle and her friends. They would make it an inviting, safe, and trusted environment, including, of course, a well-stocked refrigerator and food pantry. Their home soon became known as *Grand Central*—a place where kids could hang out, feel comfortable enough to come and go, and not be overly supervised or judged. The food pantry did the trick, and Danielle and her friends spent a great deal of their free time at the house. Leon and Debra watched each of them grow and mature as individuals, and grapple with their life's struggles. As a group, they challenged one another, shared their differing views, and encouraged each other to explore all the possibilities and opportunities available to them. During those four years, Leon and Debra had a front-row seat to the power of peers. They saw how it shaped the teens' attitudes and behavior in high school and how it affected their future. It was this group of friends who had the greatest influence on their respective decisions of where to attend college.

HOW PEERS INFLUENCE OUR SELF-CONFIDENCE

There's a great deal of research, most notably by Stanford professor emeritus Albert Bandura, that credits our peers with our level of self-confidence and self-efficacy. We build our confidence largely through social persuasion (when we are convinced by others to believe in ourselves) and social modeling (when we observe others succeeding, thus building confidence that we can also be successful).[4] UMass Boston's Dr. Carol Sharicz noted that one of the major reasons people share their knowledge with others repeatedly is because it inspires self-efficacy and improves skills. Teaching others embeds the learning in ourselves and improves our confidence because we tend to teach what we know and enjoy.

PEER ACCOUNTABILITY

Our peers not only influence us, they also hold us accountable. You may recall having had a teacher or two who understood how effective peer accountability could be. For example, if the class clown wouldn't stop disrupting the lesson, teachers who believed they had the sole power to control the situation might have said, "One more outburst and I'll send you to detention." Now, if the student didn't have anything going on that afternoon or regarded detention as a badge of honor, the laughs that would result from his next one-liner may have been worth the consequences. However, the teachers who understood that the real power rested with the group would say, "One more word out of you, young man, and the whole class will stay after school."

Both your authors have had firsthand experience as the kid on the business end of that threat, and we quickly recognized that this tactic was a game changer. No matter how funny that next one-liner might be, it would lose its luster if the whole class had to stay after school. That's something we were not willing to risk. But, how unfair, we thought. Why should the whole class be punished for our disruptive behavior? We called foul on the teachers' tactics, yet today it's hard not to admire the manner in which they put the fate of the class in our hands. If everyone had to stay after school, it would be on us. Today, we regard it as the first collateral lesson we ever received on the power of our peers.

HOW PEER INFLUENCE DRIVES LEARNING

The days of the professor standing in front of the class lecturing at a room full of silent students has given way to a facilitator model that leverages all the knowledge and talent in the room and inspires active engagement among the students. This is particularly true in graduate education (both in-person and online models), where today's students, who are often older and more experienced, participate in cohorts or learning teams. Let's look at how this change impacts the learning experience:

1. **Students engage as colleagues not competitors.** Students reap countless benefits from being part of a learning environment that stresses collaboration and abundance rather than competition.

2. **Students learn the value of dialogue.** By engaging in true dialogue, rather than debate or discussion, students participate in richer and more meaningful conversations. More listening and greater openness to varying points of view creates broader possibilities for learning outcomes.

3. **Students learn to trust one another.** The process of sharing and listening without fear of being judged builds trust. This allows for deeper, more honest conversations about beliefs and where they come from, and offers greater opportunities to learn.

4. **Students get a taste of what abundance looks like.** Students know that no matter how much they contribute to the group, they will

always get more in return and, as they do, the group only gets stronger. They actually experience a whole that is greater than the sum of its parts.

The principles outlined here also hold true in secondary education today. Secondary education expert Melissa Kelly advances this concept by differentiating between traditional working groups and cooperative learning groups. Cooperative learning groups are structured specifically to create greater student interdependence, promote individual accountability and group responsibility, allow sharing of leadership roles, improve social skills, help students learn the value of teamwork, and encourage them to engage in self and peer assessment.[5]

PEER INFLUENCE IN THE WORKPLACE

The learning evolution that's taking place in the classroom is present in our workplaces as well. Countless studies over the past twenty years reveal that learning and professional development are not just individual pursuits, they are socially constructed. Mark Knapp and John Daley, authors of the *Handbook of Interpersonal Communication,* define peer relationships as "relationships between co-workers at the same hierarchical level with no formal authority over one another."[6] These peer relationships tend to dominate the workplace because an employee will likely have one boss but several peers. Peers serve as important sources of intellectual and emotional support because they share knowledge about the workplace culture that outsiders simply do not have. They share information with one another, and they are highly influential when it comes to employee morale, job satisfaction, collaboration, and alignment.[7]

Think about the last time you announced a new strategic initiative. After delivering your speech, you returned to your office. In the meantime, team members gathered informally and engaged in a sense-making exercise aimed at clarifying what you said, what it meant for them, and how they would either embrace your ideas or simply comply with your plan. Laura Goodrich, author of *Seeing Red Cars,* says, "When sense-making happens around the water cooler, it often results in people making assumptions and engaging in banter that has little do to with propelling people to action."

Regardless of what the org chart illustrated or what your vertical structure implied, informal key influencers wielded the real power—and this is true across your organization (it's not unlike the power of the students whom the classroom teacher relied upon to quell further disruptions). However, these influencers are not always visible in an org chart, and CEOs too often miss involving and engaging them in a proper fashion.

According to Franklin Covey and its extensive research on trust, positive influences among peers improve employee engagement, build trust, and increase overall productivity. Stephen M. R. Covey explains that in the best of situations, trust among peers helps them improve as individual contributors as well as work more effectively in teams. In the worst of situations, a lack of trust among peers can poison a workplace culture and drive an organization into the ground.[8]

Ken Blanchard, author of more than fifty books on leadership, notes that up to 70 percent of all organizational change initiatives fail.[9] In a world where change is a constant, this is unacceptably high. Leaders may not be able to impose their will to achieve success, but they can create the conditions that allow employees to make their organizations successful and achieve strategic goals more often. Understanding what peer influence looks like in your organization can yield big dividends.

TRUST, CUSTOMER SERVICE, AND WHY PEERS MATTER

For the past fifteen years, the Edelman Trust Barometer has tracked public trust in institutions ranging from business and government to media and nongovernmental organizations (NGOs). The results of the 2015 global survey were sobering, as public trust in business, media, and NGOs declined, while trust in government improved only slightly. "The number of trusting countries fell to the lowest level ever recorded by the Edelman Trust Barometer, with informed publics in only six of 27 countries surveyed expressing trust levels above 60 percent."[10]

When institutions can't be trusted, people turn to their peers. It's why the Net Promoter Score (NPS) is such an effective tool for measuring customer satisfaction. Fred Reichheld, a partner at Bain & Company, created NPS in 2003 as an answer to conventional, often lengthy customer satisfaction surveys that were largely ineffective.[11]

A company's NPS is determined by obtaining the answer to what's now regarded as the ultimate question: *On a zero to ten scale, how likely is it that you would recommend us (or this product/service/brand) to a friend or colleague?*[12] Respondents are placed in one of three categories: promoters, passives, or detractors. Customers identified as promoters, who answer the question with a nine or ten, are far more likely than passives or detractors to be ambassadors (or even evangelists) for a product or service. And because people trust their peers more than their institutions, NPS is much more than a customer satisfaction metric; its purpose is to encourage company behavior that inspires and creates more promoters to drive sales. This is where NPS's real value lies, and it's just one way successful companies harness the power of peers.

HOW PEERS IMPACT US SUBCONSCIOUSLY

In 2010, *Adweek* named "Get a Mac" the best advertising campaign of the decade. As you may recall, the sixty-six spots that ran from 2006 to 2009 featured John Hodgman (I'm a PC) and Justin Long (I'm a Mac). While each commercial had a different message, the overarching question consumers were being asked was: Do you consider yourself more like the cool Mac guy or the awkward PC guy? Who would you consider your peer? The campaign ran in the United States, Australia, Canada, Japan, New Zealand, and the United Kingdom. According to Kelton Rhoads, who in 2012 analyzed the effectiveness of the campaign, Mac sales were down in 2005 and early in 2006. Once the campaign broke in the spring, sales increased by 200,000 units in the first month. By September, Apple reported a 39 percent boost in sales for the fiscal year.[13]

Apple wasn't simply selling computers; the company was inviting consumers to be part of a community with which they could proudly identify. Edward Boches, former executive creative director at Mullen, once said, "Good work tells you what a product does and why you should buy it. Great work tells you what a brand stands for and invites you to share in its beliefs." Members of the Apple community shared more than an operating system and complementary devices; they were part of something larger. They were a community of shared beliefs and sensibilities.

The research on this subject reveals that the forces at work here are powerful yet, too often, go unacknowledged. In 2008, professors Vladas Griskevicius, Robert B. Cialdini, and Noah J. Goldstein reported their findings from two fascinating experiments in *MIT Sloan Management Review.* One experiment involved observing a street musician in a New York City subway station. After getting a good measure of the percentage of passersby who stopped to listen and throw spare change in the hat, the researchers changed the conditions by planting one of their colleagues near the musician. Whenever someone would stop to listen, their colleague would reach into his pocket and toss coins into the hat. Turns out that people who witnessed someone giving money were eight times more likely to contribute than those who didn't see anyone doing so. What the researchers found most intriguing was that, when they interviewed the people who donated and asked them why they gave, those people offered every reason one could imagine except crediting, even in part, the influence of their peers. They were simply oblivious, at least consciously, to how the actions of others likely influenced their own behavior.

The second experiment offers insight into why leveraging peer messaging, as executed in the "Get a Mac" campaign, worked so effectively. In this case, the researchers left three different messages on cards in hotel rooms requesting that guests consider reusing their towels. One card said, HELP SAVE THE ENVIRONMENT, followed by information stressing respect for nature. A different card stated, PARTNER WITH US TO HELP SAVE THE ENVIRONMENT, followed by information urging guests to cooperate with the hotel in preserving the environment. A third card, using an appeal based on peer influence, said, JOIN YOUR FELLOW GUESTS IN HELPING TO SAVE

THE ENVIRONMENT, followed by information that said a majority of hotel guests reuse their towels. Which message was most effective? The peer influence appeal outperformed the other messages by 34 percent.[14]

Consistent with these experiments, the "Get a Mac" campaign didn't ask consumers if they wanted to be more productive or if they wanted to select Apple as their partner to achieve that goal. They asked them to be part of a community. And it worked.

PEER INFLUENCE ACROSS CULTURES

It shouldn't be a surprise that the "Get a Mac" campaign was successful outside the U.S. as well, because peer influence is at work in every culture in the world. In fact, peer influence plays an even larger role in countries outside North America and Western Europe.

In 1976, anthropologist Edward T. Hall created a framework for examining cultures across a spectrum of what he called high-context and low-context communication.[15] Think of a high-context culture as a tightly knit group of insiders. Here, there's a higher level of mutual understanding and, more often than not, less need for specific explanation when communicating complex ideas. In a low-context culture, cultural norms can be more divergent, and conveying anything complex requires more specific explanation.

High-context cultures tend to be more collectivist, cooperative, and team oriented, and they hold a deep respect for history and tradition. These cultures are more commonly found in Asia and the Middle East. Lower-context cultures tend to be more competitive, individualistic, and task oriented, with a future orientation and a larger appetite for change. Switzerland, Germany, the U.S., and the U.K. are considered lower-context cultures.

Richard Dool, a former CEO, Fortune 500 executive, and professor at Seton Hall University, supports Hall's findings, explaining that, based on his experience, the dynamics in Germany, the U.K., and France are all very different, but they're all still Western or lower context. "They're more individualistic than others. Now, if you look at the higher-context cultures like India, Japan, and China, they are all very different as well, but peer influence, peer respect, and peer relationships are a common theme. And I would argue they matter even more," Dool said. This concept of peer respect and peer support is deeply ingrained in high-context cultures—much more so than in the U.S. The degree and the manifestation of peer support and the way it is leveraged can be very different, but the concepts and the foundation are the same no matter where you live in the world.

WORD OF MOUTH AT SCALE

The power of peers spans all age groups, and in today's interconnected world is even more prevalent than ever. We're far less inclined to trust institutional experts than to trust the opinions and experiences of peers we've never met (peers as in fellow consumers, readers, car buyers, etc.). If a person has a bad experience with a business, he doesn't just tell a few friends, he jumps on Twitter and Yelp and tells a few million. By the start of the millennium, the level of social media engagement had grown so quickly that *Time* magazine named "You" (or "Us," I suppose) its Person of the Year in 2006.[16]

Consider popular sites such as Amazon, LinkedIn, Glassdoor, Lending Club, Angie's List, etc., as well as online communities that take various forms, from user-generated online encyclopedias (*Wikipedia*) to Q&A sites (Yahoo! Answers). In 2013, researchers Christy Cheung, Matthew Lee, and Zach Lee looked at the unprecedented amount of collaboration that takes place in the world today through online communities and posed questions that sought to understand why people share so willingly and for such long durations.[17] Using an online survey, they found that when people received the level of reciprocity they expected, they were satisfied and continued to share. They also learned that when people believed their knowledge was truly benefiting others, it improved their self-efficacy and, in turn, their satisfaction. If both these outcomes are realized, members of the community are more likely to continue contributing and sharing their knowledge. This dynamic is essential to the life cycle of these communities, as they can remain intact even as individual members come and go.

HOW PEERS INFLUENCE WINNING

One organization that has demonstrated an extraordinary peer-to-peer cultural dynamic is the University of Connecticut women's basketball team. In 2015, the team won its tenth national championship in a span of twenty years, and every player who has gone through the program since 1988 has appeared in at least one Final Four.

In April of 2015, statistician and writer Nate Silver dubbed UConn the most dominant college basketball team on earth, citing an eighty-four-game stretch that included an average margin of victory of thirty-eight points per game.[18] During the 2014–15 season, head coach Geno Auriemma and assistant coach Chris Dailey, who has been with the program since Auriemma came to Connecticut in 1985, received accolades for securing their 900th victory and another national championship.

The question everyone continues to ask is: What makes UConn so dominant? There are other terrific coaches and great players at top programs—Notre Dame, Stanford, and South Carolina, to name a few. Why is this team consistently so much better? While Auriemma may be regarded among the best to ever coach the game on any level, and the school's winning program allows it to recruit great players, he admits that this is not what makes Connecticut perform at such a consistently high level. Instead, Auriemma has suggested that the difference stems from UConn's culture and having highly competitive players who are uniquely committed to one another and are willing to sacrifice individual objectives for team goals.

UConn assistant coach and former player Shea Ralph described this culture in more detail. She explained that a few years ago, Bria Hartley, an All-American as a sophomore, was not having a strong junior year. Heading into the NCAA tournament, the team had lost more games than it typically does in a season. "We knew we had to make a change," Shea said. According to Shea, Coach Auriemma called a meeting and said, "These are the things that have been happening with our team, and we have to change something. We have to get better. I need you guys to tell me what you think would make us better." Bria responded, "Coach, I think it would be best if I came off the bench."

Shea noted:

That's the kind of players we have. And we won the National Championship that year. Even if coming off the bench really wasn't what Bria wanted, she knew that's what the team needed. I don't know that as a freshman she would've ever been capable of doing that, but because of the support of her teammates and her coaches, she learned about winning, sacrifice, and what it takes to be a great teammate.

When other players on the team see an All-American make that kind of sacrifice, it makes them want to win for that player. So whether players are not feeling well and continue to push themselves through practice or a game, or you watch an All-American dive on the floor for a loose ball, sacrificing personal goals is an everyday part of our culture. It inspires the younger player to ask herself, "Is that something that I do every day? Is that something that I'm willing to do every day?" It creates a mindset that we're all in the same boat. Our players know that they have to be there for each other.

HAVING THE SUPPORT OF A TEAM

Training for a marathon takes four to five months of hard work, assuming you're in pretty good shape before you even start. For a first-time marathoner, it involves running four or five days a week, starting at roughly fifteen miles per week and peaking at about forty miles a week as the race gets closer, depending on the training program. Achieving this goal without the support of a group or a "team," as Team In Training's Bruce Cleland calls it, is clearly not impossible. People do it. But for many of the first-time marathoners who completed the race by working with Team In Training, the knowledge, encouragement, and support they received from their team members was invaluable. If they didn't feel accountable to their fellow runners or to the organization, many of the runners may have either slacked on their training or not run the race at all. Most marathoners will tell you that the race isn't nearly as challenging as the discipline it takes to train for eighteen consecutive weeks to prepare for it. That's where you need the most support.

SUMMARY

Whether it's in school, at work, or in sports, our peers matter. Sometimes we see their influence right in front of our faces. Other times, it's evident in ways we don't necessarily recognize or acknowledge. If you're a CEO or business owner, consider this: no matter where people work or go to school in this world, peer influence—whether it's overt or subconscious, and whether it takes place in person or online—is a force that cannot be ignored. Your peers are critical to your success and happiness. They include everyone from the colleagues you see every day to perfect strangers with whom you share a common interest at a moment in time. The peers in your organization also wield enormous power and influence among your employees. It's for these reasons that business leaders at any level cannot ignore the power and pervasive nature of peer influence.

In our next chapter, we'll zero in on four primary ways people engage their peers and make the case for why CEOs need to understand what it will mean for them when they *accelerate*.

3

The Path to Peer Advantage

Many of us participate in the four basic methods of peer engagement—connect, network, optimize, and accelerate—simultaneously and through various methods. Connecting and networking tend to be individual pursuits that leverage peer influence from a higher volume of peers with less structure to the interaction. Accelerating and optimizing are group efforts that create what we call *peer advantage*, which by definition is more strategic and structured in nature.

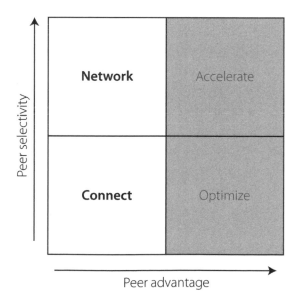

FIGURE 3.1   Peer Engagement Framework: Connect and Network

You may have already connected today with peers on Facebook or LinkedIn or in a group meeting. When people connect, they tend to:

- Exchange information
- Extend their reach by introducing themselves to more people
- Contribute to the conversation, yet rely on the participation of others to realize value
- Share a common interest during a given period of time
- Rely on a high volume of peers they don't know
- Share with others in an open, yet unsecure environment that lacks privacy or safety
- Participate when they choose; it's optional

DEAN ACOSTA CONNECTS

Dean Acosta, an Emmy Award–winning former journalist and press secretary for NASA, has led corporate communication teams at several Fortune 500 companies and is now global head of corporate communications and media for Phillips 66. Like many people, he accesses websites to exchange information with peers with whom he may share interests and to stay close to his friends. In a professional context, Dean also works extensively with colleagues and competitors in a manner that improves everyone's professional acumen.

Dean connects in different ways for different reasons. "I don't think I buy anything online without reading reviews and looking at other people's comments. My wife, Trish, and I don't hire a contractor without checking Yelp. When we want to dine out at a new restaurant, we tend to rely on reviews from Open Table. And since we purchase just about everything on Amazon, we count on the prevailing sentiment of consumer reviews there to inform our buying decisions," Dean said.

On Facebook, Dean stays connected with many of his fellow Seton Hall University graduate school alums to stay abreast of how they are progressing in their careers, and he keeps in touch with his former NASA colleagues, who keep him apprised of what's happening in the space program. Here on earth, staying connected helps Dean get to work on time. "I'm using the Waze app right now for traffic, as I drive to work. Waze has got input from drivers saying, 'Hey, I just saw a police officer or there's a pothole up here.' I get these notices as I'm driving along, and it helps me to navigate my path, avoid traffic, maybe even avoid a flat tire from hitting a pothole."

Dean is also active in the Arthur W. Page Society, a professional association for senior public relations and corporate communications executives, and is a member of a group called Page Up. Dean said, "Page Up has done this really great job of creating this share point, where everybody has a profile and they engage in open dialogue and knowledge sharing. There's a weekly Thursday online gathering, where we'll pose a question or we'll answer questions."

When Dean began to assume responsibility for financial communications at Phillips 66, he tapped this group for their knowledge and ideas. "I had a couple of things I was looking to do. I shared these ideas simply by putting them out there. Here's what I'm thinking, what do you guys think? I got some great feedback." Dean found the dialogue extremely helpful. While he knew some of the group participants and valued their opinions, there were others he didn't know at all, but since many of them represented Fortune 50 companies, their opinions carried a great deal of weight.

During Dean's time as NASA's press secretary, he participated in a similar group that was pulled together organically and later called the Coalition for Space Exploration. It included industry representatives of all the companies that worked with NASA. In this gathering of communication professionals, the members discovered an easy mechanism for talking about ways they could engage audiences outside the industry and inspire the general public. Their idea exchange would not only support NASA but also serve as a forum for sharing best practices they could apply to their organizations. Dean said that this forum resulted in his making lifelong friends, and that it inspired his active involvement in the Arthur Page Society.

Later, as Phillips 66's representative for the American Petroleum Institute (API), Dean became an active member of the communication council. Here, representatives and peers from communication departments in the biggest energy companies in the world collaborate and share ideas. Dean participates in monthly meetings at which industry participants discuss issues and methods for communicating and educating various stakeholder groups. Dean said, "I find it as valuable, if not more so, than when I was in the space industry, because we're able to have a better understanding of how Chevron approaches its work or how ExxonMobil does it. I find myself bringing a lot of these learnings back to my team and my company."

As you can see, connecting runs the gamut from sharing personal and professional information, and asking people whom you've never met for their take on products and services, to engaging peers more selectively in information exchanges about best practices. By and large, people connect with peers who are relevant to their demographic, interests, industry, and roles. Connecting is quick and convenient. The critical mass of successful communities keeps them self-sustaining and, as a result, the demands and expectations of individual participants tend to be low because the sheer number of participants helps maintain a strong level of activity. The lack of structure and anonymity may contribute to experiences that are less consistent than those people have when they network, optimize, or accelerate, but it's hard to argue with the overall value of connecting.

Connecting and staying connected has never been easier. Some of us crave connection while admittedly others may not. No matter which is true for you, its power is undeniable both for the individual and for the community at large. Let's explore the order of peer engagement beyond making connections, one that tends to be even more purposeful and meaningful. Let's look at why we network.

NETWORKING: IT'S ALL ABOUT PURPOSEFUL RELATIONSHIPS

To network is to value the power of personal relationships to achieve individual goals—yours and those of others in your network. Networkers seek out peers and associate with peer groups who can help them get jobs, recruit clients, create business partnerships, etc. If you consider the phrase "It's not what you know, it's who you know" a bit of an overstatement, think again. We interviewed business leaders from around the world who told us unequivocally that when it comes to getting a job or building a client base, personal networks have never been more essential.

You **network** online and at conferences, or at local business events and socials, in a more selective and more purposeful attempt to advance personal and professional interests. When people network, they tend to:

- Not only exchange information but work with others to create opportunities (jobs, business partnerships, financing, etc.)
- Select peers based on specific, qualifying criteria (from medium to high value)
- Recommend peers to others based on trust
- Work with peers toward achieving a singular goal
- Understand there's a higher degree of expected reciprocity
- Enjoy a moderately safer environment for exposing vulnerability
- Realize that participation is optional

The term networking has become somewhat trivialized, largely because people have come to associate it with schmoozing at events or exchanging pleasantries and business cards. Those who do it well, however, understand its real value. Just look back at your own career. Consider the many times you received help or offered assistance to others by facilitating personal introductions. It's anything but trivial. It can change lives.

Jimmy Fallon credits networking for his rise from a struggling stand-up comic in Hollywood to a star on *Saturday Night Live* and eventually host of the *Tonight Show*. At first, Fallon benefited from LA entertainment agent Randi Siegel's contacts, which got him two auditions for *Saturday Night Live*. After bombing the first audition, he got a second and joined the *SNL* cast in 1998, where he worked hard to build a strong relationship with Lorne Michaels. After Conan O'Brien left *Late Night*, Michaels tapped Fallon for the job. While there, Fallon reached out to Jay Leno for advice and continued to strengthen his network. Fallon essentially earned a great deal of respect because he was a good listener, a true student of comedy, and so respectful of others. Fallon's ability to network was not only a key ingredient of his promotion to host of the *Tonight Show* in February 2014, it has also helped him attract a superb lineup of guests who fuel the show's amazing success.[1]

NETWORKING IS CONNECTING ON A PURPOSEFUL LEVEL

Networking is about building relationships that involve either an implied or stated reciprocity—the same reciprocity that makes a community vibrant and self-sustaining is also the cornerstone of the individual relationships we create for our personal networks. Brian Solis, best-selling author and Altimeter Group principal, told us that reciprocity is the underlying currency for people who connect and network most effectively. "The biggest lesson about reciprocity is that you recognize it as something that's earned. Doing so involves providing value to someone else without an obvious quid pro quo," Solis said. It simply requires us to be selfless in the pursuit of self-interest.

When you do something for someone without expecting to receive anything in return, you're saying that you care about the other person and the relationship you share. No matter what your personal expectations, the relationship (personal or professional) is paramount. If you approach networking in that way, you're far more likely to achieve better individual outcomes—and help others do the same—far more often. Why? Because we live in a world where we need each other. Time and time again, we've seen that once individuals become more concerned with giving value than receiving it, and they discover others doing the same, they are drawn into a powerful reinforcing cycle. This dynamic is so well recognized that there are countless organizations dedicated to helping people build their personal networks.

Consider the thousands of women who join Ellevate, a global networking group of businesswomen who share best practices, attend events, and learn from one another. Sallie Krawcheck, who rebranded the organization from 85 Broads to Ellevate, describes networking as the number-one unwritten rule of success in business. With thirty-four thousand members across the globe, Ellevate uses networking to inspire peer-to-peer learning and encourage women to invest in the success of other women.

Young Presidents' Organization (YPO) is another example of an enterprise that brings CEOs and business owners together in powerful ways. By participating in high-end business and social events, members connect in a manner that breaks down barriers and cultivates new working relationships. Formal networking takes place outside YPO as part of an initiative the organization calls meetings-in-meetings. YPO member Bernie Tenenbaum, who joined the YPO New Jersey Chapter in 1994, describes the program, which launched twenty years ago, this way: "We didn't set out to create meetings-in-meetings in YPO. The concept started as an accident in the way that all great ideas start."[2]

A YPO meeting-in-meeting connects members already attending an industry trade show or major entertainment or sporting event, and gives them the opportunity to meet and network behind the scenes. There are more than one hundred meetings-in-meetings every year. "The event is the paradigm of education and idea exchange," says Tenenbaum. "It has provided opportunities for people to do business with each other, to seek advice, and deals get done."[3]

GOING SOCIAL FOR AMPLIFIED NETWORKING

Just as connecting has become more immediate and more convenient, social media's less time-consuming and less expensive attributes serve as the perfect networking complement to attending live events. Social media not only affords us the opportunity to network online, but also helps us more easily extend live event experiences well past the events themselves. We've seen it firsthand at several LinkedIn events we've attended over the years. After the event, the attendees will reach out to new people they met and extend a hand to those they didn't. And attending the same event opens the door to further conversation and networking long after participants return home. A look at online participation in Canada revealed that, in addition to networking at live events, 63 percent of respondents are networking on LinkedIn and 61 percent on Facebook.[4] This may explain in part why LinkedIn CEO Jeff Weiner is so passionate about his vision for LinkedIn as a leader in building a thriving global economy.

Weiner sees the role and potential of his company more broadly and clearly than many of its members. And it's all about networking. In the summer of 2015, at a LinkedIn conference in San Francisco, Weiner restated what he calls the company's economic graph, which was created to digitally represent and map the global economy. His vision is that all of the world's three billion workers will have a LinkedIn profile and that every company and not-for-profit organization in the world will have a profile as well. He wants a digital representation of every available job, whether it's a full-time, part-time, temporary, or volunteer position. He wants every skill that's required to do those jobs represented digitally, and every education organization and learning development resource that can help someone acquire those skills to be visible on the platform as well. To the extent that people, organizations, and education institutions wish to share their knowledge, they can create an environment where knowledge and identity are intertwined, and where it will be just as easy for opportunities to find a member as it is for a member to find opportunities.

Best-selling author and Altimeter Group principal Charlene Li notes, "For professionals, LinkedIn is the default place to go to connect and network.... In the past, LinkedIn was just a profile site. Now it offers ways for you to express who you are and what you care about, and to build relationships that can result in everything from obtaining a job to finding a business partner."

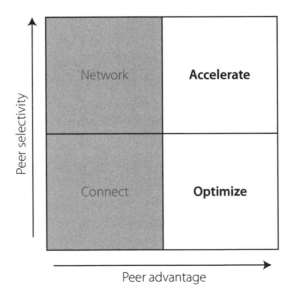

FIGURE 3.2　Peer Engagement Framework: Optimize and Accelerate

OPTIMIZING GROWTH

If you've ever witnessed a live performance of the U.S. Navy's flight demonstration squadron, the Blue Angels, it's not likely that you forgot how they took your breath away. The sound alone goes right through you, and your eyes can hardly believe what they're seeing. During their demonstrations, six pilots, selected from the navy and the marines, fly their F/A-18 Hornets into formations in which, at times, they are traveling one hundred feet off the ground at five hundred miles per hour and only eighteen inches apart.

With the margin for error so slight and the smallest mistake likely to be disastrous, you wonder how these pilots do what they do so consistently. Former U.S. Marine Corps F/A-18 Hornet instructor pilot Patrick Houlahan said, "These are the best pilots in the world, and what's most remarkable about their precision and safety record year-in and year-out is that they achieve it with a flight team that's constantly changing." Pat reminded us that it's not only about having world-class pilots. What makes the Blue Angels stand out is that they have processes that are beyond reproach. A major part of what allows the Blue Angels to perform as they do involves a process called the debrief—an excellent example of what we call *optimizing*.

After every Blue Angels flight, whether it's a practice or a performance, the pilots meet for a debrief session. Keep in mind that, from the perspective of the Blue Angels, there is no such thing as a perfect flight. As a result, pilots review every aspect of what they do, down to the smallest detail, including evaluating their salutes and their marches to and from the jets. During the debrief, pilots take turns talking about the errors they made and make firm commitments to the team that the errors will be fixed next time. The process requires acknowledgment and a commitment among peers to getting better with each and every flight.

Another essential aspect of debriefing, especially in an organization where rank is so important, is that the meetings are conducted in a manner that gives equal footing to everyone. No matter their age, experience, or rank, debrief participants are free to say what has to be said for the good of the squadron without fear of repercussion. What happens in the meeting stays in the meeting. Pat said, "It's not about who is right, it's about what is right."

At the start of the season, a maneuver that features planes flying eighteen inches apart begins with pilots practicing at forty-five feet apart. During the early months, debrief sessions take as long as four hours. As the flights improve and the planes fly closer and closer together, debriefs typically take about two hours. Pat told us that by the time these pilots get to the end of their eight-month season and they have those planes eighteen inches apart, the debrief takes roughly fifteen minutes. Optimizing is about chasing perfection in the pursuit of excellence.

WHAT IT MEANS TO OPTIMIZE IN BUSINESS

Leaders who optimize in the business world participate in company or industry-specific peer groups to achieve goals such as improving collaboration, achieving alignment, and deepening team knowledge of company or industry issues. They also use these groups to augment executive development programs.

You **optimize** when you work together in teams to bring a high level of excellence to achieving a common goal. As we have seen, leaders often form organizational "tiger teams" to tackle special projects; the Blue Angels conduct debriefs following every (what we see as perfect) flight to talk about how they can do better the next time; and top sports teams participate in practices that are often more rigorous than the games to ensure top performance when it truly counts. The work of optimizing tends to take place among a more homogenous group of peers, and to be temporary in nature, determined by either the length of a specific project or the span of a season. People who optimize tend to:

- Work as part of a group committed to achieving a collective goal, often a desire to move from good to great
- Work in small to midsized groups or teams
- Engage in an environment where it is moderately safe to share exactly what's on their minds
- Buy into the structure of the group as well as the collective goal
- Realize that participation is not optional, it's essential

Certain organizations have learned how to optimize a peer feedback loop to improve business processes, research, and organizational insight. At Gartner, the global IT research and advisory company, research analysts participate in structured peer review of their research by releasing a "stalking horse" position into the analyst community. The company benefits when the content is examined by analysts with differing viewpoints, forcing the authoring analyst to refine, test, and adjust her conclusion multiple times until it is defensible to clients. People who work together to optimize don't simply participate in the learning process, they drive an overall standard of excellence because they help one another better. Equifax, for example, uses optimizer groups by creating cross-functional work teams to open lines of communication, improve collaboration, and assure organizational alignment.

HOW TO ACCELERATE GROWTH

When Gerry, CEO of a professional services firm based in the Midwest, wanted to make a major change in the way he charged and invoiced his clients, moving from an hourly billing rate to an overall project fee, he developed a plan based on input from his local CEO peer advisory group and set off a paradigm shift in his local market. To pressure test the idea, he took his plan to his national industry-networking group. They summarily shot it down. "No one in the industry does it that way because it's too difficult to get paid for the hours worked when the scope of work changes," one member said. The others echoed this response in various forms.

Later, he returned to his CEO peer advisory group, which was made up of CEOs from a wide range of industry sectors, to discuss his industry group's objections, only to be reminded that his idea, while unheard of in his industry, had been implemented quite successfully in other sectors. "Go for it," they said. The CEO group concluded that the plan was sound; the industry trade group simply lacked imagination in this particular case. They were trapped in their own silo. Gerry implemented his plan with resounding success because his clients had greater certainty about the overall costs of the project (up front) and a clear understanding of what would trigger cost increases. Gerry's regional competitors were left with one option: to follow Gerry's lead.

While industry-specific peer groups can be extremely valuable, people typically join them because they assume they will learn more and receive the best advice from those who already understand the nuances of their business. In Gerry's case, the advice he received from a more diverse set of peers who were not blinded by industry norms made the difference between succeeding and failing. This is similar to the story we shared earlier about Paul Caskey's seasonality problem with hair bleaching powders in the cosmetics industry. A common practice in one industry may be completely foreign to another. In Gerry's group, he gets asked the tough questions by peers who face similar challenges but address them in very different ways. Leadership expert Simon Sinek once said that stepping out of your industry silo is one of the most effective ways of coming up with something new.[5]

As stated earlier, while optimizing tends to take place in the same company or industry for finite periods of time, the essence of accelerating is realized in the diversity of the group and the longevity of the group experience. People who accelerate tend to:

- Be very particular about surrounding themselves with people who share their passion and determination toward achieving a specific goal
- Understand the importance of engaging with peers who have points of view and experiences different from their own
- Commit to helping others and by doing so helping themselves
- Appreciate the unexpected, positive outcomes that can be realized by engaging in deep discussion
- Value having a safe and confidential environment where they are free to share both their aspirations and their fears
- Accept that participation is mandatory and that members hold one another accountable for what they do inside and outside the group meetings

To accelerate is to help members achieve individual goals, rather than the shared goals pursued by groups created to optimize. Here, a CEO from a bank works side by side with peers who may run the local hospital, advertising agency, and manufacturing company. While the very concept of peer diversity may feel like a contradiction, broadening the definition of "peer" allows you to consider the value of working with people from different backgrounds and industries.

GETTING UNCOMFORTABLE

Leaders who challenge themselves to accelerate embark on a journey of personal and professional growth that stretches them out of their comfort zone into a landscape that is unfamiliar yet rich with learning opportunities. Ken Mueller, president of Mueller Die Cut Solutions, leveraged his peer advisory group to resolve a tricky business challenge: six of the eight managers in his China facility threatened to quit if he did not fire the general manager. Ken knew that the way he handled the situation would determine whether production continued uninterrupted and the facility operated smoothly over the long term. Because Ken's business partners shared his limited experience managing this type of delicate personnel issue in Asia, he needed insight from a select group of peers who had managed similar issues. And he needed expert guidance to help extract that insight for maximum benefit. What's more, every executive present during the discussion would learn from the way Ken processed his issue.

Ken's CEO peer advisory group helped him accelerate his ability to manage a challenging situation, prompting him to fly to China, personally listen to each team member, and craft a three-month transition plan, which included replacing 75 percent of the management team and eventually the general manager.

PEER ADVANTAGE: WHY IT WORKS

One of the most powerful dynamics of groups designed to optimize and accelerate is the momentum created when peers engage in a cycle of learning, sharing, applying, and achieving. The individual pursuits of connecting and networking can produce remarkable outcomes, but to improve your chances of realizing a level of excellence that will set you apart from the pack, you need something more. You need to participate in a highly select peer group that is both structured in its framework and strategic in its approach to achieving the personal goals you share with your group members. Whether group members are executives with different skill sets from the same organization (optimize) or CEOs collaborating with fellow CEOs from entirely different industries and backgrounds (accelerate), they participate in a process that by its nature fuels continuous improvement.

To capture the essence of why groups that optimize and accelerate are so effective we need to understand the powerful reinforcing loop these group experiences create.

Learning—It's the first stage of the process and, for too many organizations, it's the last. Peter Senge describes the learning organization as one "where people continually expand their capacity to create the results they truly desire, where new and expansive patterns of thinking are nurtured, where collective aspiration is set free, and where people

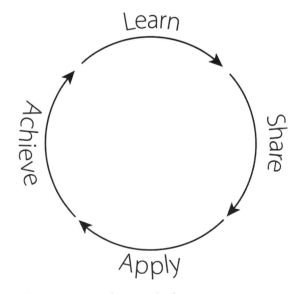

FIGURE 3.3 The Learning–Achieving Cycle

are learning how to learn together."[6] He also suggests that we wouldn't claim to know how to ride a bicycle if we only rode the bike one time. Learning is about demonstrating the capacity to produce quality results repeatedly. It's the difference between riding a bike and being a bicycle rider. Peer groups (whether they evolve naturally or are created purposely) serve as a mechanism to create bicycle riders by fostering the application of deep learning through collaboration.

Sharing—Whether knowledge is gained from reading a book or attending an offsite training program, sharing it delivers value to our peers and colleagues and, in our role as teacher or conveyor, helps us embed what we've learned. Peers not only engage in rich dialogue about cutting-edge concepts, they tend to ask hard questions and challenge one another to tackle complex issues using their newfound knowledge. Peers reinforce and essentially give one another permission to try new ways of working.

Applying—It's hard to overstress the importance of applying what you've learned. This is where the sports practice metaphor comes into play. The best of the best don't rely on talent alone to excel or win championships. UConn's players will tell you that their practices are much tougher than their games. They take what they learn and apply it until it becomes second nature. Peer groups hold individuals accountable for practicing their craft and fine-tuning news ways of working. This peer-to-peer accountability is essential to the success of this stage in the reinforcing loop.

Achieving—Good behaviors will replace bad ones, but only over time and after repeated success. Achieving inspires believing. Believing in yourself and growing to trust a newfound way of working fuels the hunger to learn more, and the cycle continues. Achieving also inspires others to emulate your behavior. Leadership experts Jim Kouzes and Barry Posner call it "modeling the way."[7] As a CEO you can model the way for your peers and your employees and, as a leader in a company, you can do the same. It's about walking the talk and others following your lead.

HOW TO CREATE PEER ADVANTAGE

If realizing true peer advantage were as simple as starting or joining a group of peers, there wouldn't be much point in continuing. The prevailing best practices, carefully honed over time, that drive high-quality CEO peer advisory groups served to inform our model of learning, sharing, applying, and achieving, and to identify the five factors necessary for accessing peer advantage. Being selective, structured, and strategic in a group setting may offer some guidance for the difference between peer influence and peer advantage, but it leaves far too much to the imagination. The five factors offer you the details. We dedicate a full chapter to each factor, but in short form, here are the **five factors for peer advantage** and why they matter.

Select the right peers—This involves more than surrounding yourself with the right people. Based on your personal and professional goals, it requires reflection on whether you are well suited for a group experience, whether a particular group is right for you, and how you know if your group is providing you with true peer advantage.

Create a safe environment—Deep conversations about critical intellectual and emotional issues require an environment in which confidentiality is sacrosanct and you never feel you're being judged. We'll talk about how this environment is created and why it's so crucial.

Utilize a smart guide—Whether a group is led by a member or a professional facilitator, maximizing the potential of any group depends on great leadership. We tapped the experience of some of the world's best CEO peer advisory group leaders to learn more about how they lead their groups for optimal peer advantage.

Foster valuable interaction—Having a safe environment is an essential first step, but strategies that help members achieve their goals and processes that help direct conversations to what really matters doesn't happen by accident—it happen by design.

Be accountable—If you're a member of a group that optimizes and accelerates well, the group members don't tell you what you should do, you tell them what you plan to do. Once you do that, you not only own the solution, your fellow members will expect you to do what you say you will do (DWYSYWD). This level of group accountability gives peer advantage its punctuation.

SUMMARY

People, generally speaking, connect more than they network. They network more than they optimize and optimize more than they accelerate. CEOs, whose time is extremely valuable, should invest their energy in these peer engagement activities in the opposite order they were presented: they should accelerate, optimize, network, and connect.

Why? Invest your time where you get the most value, like any good CEO does. It's essential that you get out of your company and industry silos to engage in rich conversations with a diverse group of fellow CEOs who truly empathize with the magnitude of your responsibility. Ask any high-performing CEO in a group. Your peers will broaden and deepen your knowledge and help you lead your organization more effectively. Next, optimize. Take what you learn from your CEO group—your ideas and your understanding about how high-performing groups collaborate—and show your people how to lead groups that optimize inside your organization. Networking involves purposeful interaction with select individuals who can help you and your organization grow. What you gain from accelerating and optimizing will help you be an even more purposeful and successful networker. Finally, stay connected. Connecting helps extend your reach and provides you with an additional knowledge channel for intentional and collateral learning.

PART II

The Five Factors for Peer Advantage

4

Select the Right Peers

Surrounding yourself with the right people is essential to achieving peer advantage. However, when it comes to finding peers who will help you accelerate, ask yourself two questions: Is a specific peer advisory group right for you, and will you be a good fit for the group? It has to be a win–win. This involves exploring how well you may be suited to giving and receiving value in this kind of forum. Peer advantage doesn't come cheap, but if you share strong group values, set clear goals, commit yourself to the other members by giving and receiving, and appreciate all the benefits, there's no limit to what you can accomplish.

SHARED VALUES THAT MATTER

Finding the ideal CEO peer advisory group, or starting one of your own, involves asking, "How will I identify which peers can really help me?" To answer that question, it's important to look beyond a prospective member's title and credentials. Consider the way you approach hiring an employee to join your company. The person who ultimately wins the job doesn't just have the technical skills to do the work; she is likely a good cultural fit for your organization. The same holds true whether you're creating or joining a CEO peer advisory group. While these groups can be aptly compared to snowflakes, because there are no two that are exactly the same, good peer advisory groups do share a set of beliefs in the pursuit of common goals. Following are seven shared beliefs that are essential for any successful group.

The Group Is Smarter Than Any One Individual

As the CEO, you may not always be the smartest one in the room, but at the office you're often treated that way because you are the ultimate decision maker. Transitioning from a setting where you hold a top position to a setting where you are one among equals involves recognizing your fellow CEOs as colleagues and understanding that the collective experience in the room is greater than that of any individual member.

According to Dave Logan, coauthor of *Tribal Leadership*, this can be a difficult transition, especially for those CEOs who lead workplaces that he describes as having "Stage Three" cultures. Logan noted that his research revealed that 50 percent of companies live in a state of Stage Three, where the theme is "I'm great, and you're not." In this type of culture knowledge is power, so people tend to hoard it, and winning is not only everything, it's personal.[1]

Dave has been working with CEO peer groups for years. He remembers one CEO describing his transition this way: "At first, I thought obviously there's something wrong with the people in my company, because if I had really great people in my company, like the people in my group, I'd have a better company. Then I began to realize that by thinking I always had to be the best, I was actually diminishing my team." Years later, while working with CCI, an organization that runs CEO peer advisory groups for Fortune 1000 companies, Dave had lunch with a CEO (also a PhD in physics) who ran a Fortune 500 tech company, and he heard the same type of comment: "I assumed I was the best. I came into this group, and it was this transformational experience. I realized it was my job to take that back and build the same culture in my executive team as I have in my CCI group."

Once you believe in the collective knowledge of the group and that you are simply one among equals, you can participate as a full member, and when you go back to work, you can help your employees realize their potential as well. You see your group meeting not as a place to judge but as a place to learn.

Leaders Benefit from Insightful Questions and Advice from Their Peers

As Paul Caskey surmised in chapter 1, his CEO peer advisory group was the place he got his answers questioned rather than his questions answered. The group setting is where you'll be asked the hard questions—questions from people who know what it's like to sit in the CEO's chair, are blind to sacred cows, and have no tangible self-interest in the outcome. Your fellow members may really care about your success, but they have no skin in the game. They ask unfiltered questions and offer impartial advice that not only help you pressure test your own answers, but also explore new ways of thinking.

Using Logan's model for the Five Stages of Culture as a framework, high-performing CEO peer advisory groups perform at the Stage Four or Stage Five level.[2] In Stage Four, members focus on their aspirations and work together both inside and outside their group meetings to help one another achieve maximum impact. Over time, they become so effective at asking questions and offering advice that Stage Five becomes possible. In Stage Five, the group moves beyond conversations about best practices and helps you focus your attention on innovation, your vision for the future, and how to inspire people to realize their full potential. You don't see the world in terms of being better than your competitor; you view it as setting your own standard of excellence—for yourself and your organization.

Bob Duncan leads a high-performing CEO peer advisory group in New York that he described as "armed and dangerous." Duncan said:

> We go far beyond our typical model of monthly meetings and one-to-one coaching sessions. The members get together on their own, without my being involved at all, where they continue to ask the tough questions and offer sound advice. They gather in small groups for breakfast, share various thought leadership articles with one another, and even work together in tiger teams (small groups of CEOs who will assist a member with implementing a strategy). Andy, who is one of my members, promised the group he would start a new program at his company.

Realizing that Andy could use some hands-on assistance to get it done, several group members went to his business, where they all rolled up their sleeves and made it happen.

Great questions and unfettered advice and feedback help members build trust and extend their relationships beyond the group meeting. Everyone who engages in this exchange fully reaps the benefits of peer advantage.

Leaders, Regardless of Industry Sector, Share Aspirations and Challenges

CEOs may lead companies in fields that range from health care and banking to manufacturing and tech. Their industries may vary greatly but their challenges do not. They deal with financial issues, marketing challenges, and human resource problems, just like everybody else. They want to craft the best strategies, attract the best talent, and create cultures of innovation in this fast-changing world.

Nicole Mouskondis, co-CEO of Nicholas and Company, a $600 million food service distributor based in Salt Lake City, Utah, is involved in a number of peer advisory groups, where she sees the similarities across industries far more than the differences. Nicole said that working with a number of groups, particularly those outside her industry, gave her and her co-CEO, Peter, the courage to hire senior-level executives from outside the food service industry. "For years, we would watch high-level leaders jump from one food distributor to another distributor—from Sysco to U.S. Food Service to somewhere else, or vice versa. Then, about ten years ago, Peter and I actually started thinking to ourselves, 'What would it look like if we hired somebody from a different industry, with a different mindset and different perspective?'"

As Nicole described it, Nicholas and Company was among the first, if not the first, to hire executive-level talent from outside of the food distribution industry. And when they did, their industry peers said, "What are you doing? Why would you hire someone with no food service experience?"

Nicole said, "He didn't have food experience, but he had distribution experience. He understands how to move a box from A to B. He doesn't understand the food; he'll get that, but he really understands the logistics piece." Later, they hired other senior-level people from outside the industry and it's given the company a very different mindset. Mixing new employees with the people who've been at Nicholas for a long time has been a booster shot for the company because they are learning so much from one another. This brand of team learning is making the company stronger as it's implementing news ways of working. As Nicole and Peter now know, people from diverse industries have more similarities than they have differences.

Leaders Can Benefit from Reaching Outside Their Industry Sector

Because CEOs share common challenges, it stands to reason that there are specific strategies for meeting them that may be commonplace in one industry yet unheard of in another. As we discussed in chapter 4, Gerry experienced it firsthand when he changed his invoicing to a method that was outside industry norms. Had he not looked outside his industry, he never would have been introduced to new ways of working with his clients.

Nicole Mouskondis of Nicholas and Company, who added senior people to her executive leadership team from outside the food distribution industry, also talks about how they have fundamentally changed the manner in which the co-CEOs think about the business. "Our executive vice president, Dave Robbins, is a good example. He spent seventeen years in the logistics industry, working for CR England, which is North America's largest refrigerated truck carrier. They're a huge organization. Dave brought us a whole new way of thinking about our business—in terms of profitability, efficiency, and labor-engineered standards." Nicole said that before Dave came on board, the company didn't have project management, to speak of, inside the organization. With the opening of a new Las Vegas Distribution Center and an ERP implementation that is ongoing, she learned that the company needed subject matter experts. "Had Dave not come on board, we wouldn't have appreciated the value of having subject matter experts who understand the business and the functionality of equipment and software. In the past, we've always looked at our software as an IT issue. Today, we see it as a business issue."

This is why sharing ideas and practices across industries can be so powerful and why you can learn so much from CEOs who lead organizations that are completely different from your own.

People Prefer to Implement Their Own Solutions

There's a fundamental difference between what you get from a consulting firm and what you receive from a CEO peer advisory group. Both are valuable resources, but here's the difference: when you receive recommendations from a consulting firm, you are left to implement their ideas. In some cases, you can adopt these recommendations and implement them as if they were your own, but it many cases that simply doesn't happen. In a CEO group, you are challenged to take note of what you've learned from your colleagues and make a commitment to developing and implementing your own solutions.

Marshall Goldsmith coaches CEOs to refrain from adding too much value to the ideas presented by their employees because once a CEO adds to an idea, the employees no longer see it as their own. As a result, Goldsmith explains, commitment to its execution, even when the employees themselves planted the seed of the idea, can be reduced by as much as 50 percent.[3] The same holds true when outside consultants deliver recommendations to their clients. The quality of the ideas may be outstanding, but all too often the plans fail miserably in the execution stage because there's no emotional tie to their success. The point here isn't about whose idea or approach is best, it's about whose recommendations get implemented successfully more often. A CEO who owns a particular strategy and announces a plan to implement it to the group tends to be more committed to doing so successfully.

Success Is Often the Best Teacher

When something works better, you are more inclined to adopt it. Until then, because you don't trust it fully, your tentative commitment becomes a precursor for lack of adoption. Success drives the willingness to change. By practicing and mastering best practices that you learn with your colleagues, you can take these practices to your own organization with the confidence that they'll achieve your desired outcomes.

Christopher Lee, CEO of the Memphis-based multicultural marketing firm Think Inspired, said that his first real experience with working in a peer group was as a member of a learning team in graduate school—he attended a hybrid program (in-person and online) for a master of arts in strategic communication and leadership from Seton Hall University. Throughout the program, Chris worked with the same learning team, a group of mid- to senior-level executives from across the country, whom he engaged primarily online. Over the course of eighteen months, he and his learning team members were often handed assignments that involved working in small groups of three or four students—they submitted their work as a team, to be graded as a team. Chris found himself working with people who approached their work very differently from the way he did. Chris said, "There were some people who I initially found very hard to trust that they were going to do their part. Turns out, out of all my group projects, everyone did what they said they were going to do. Everyone delivered. I think that forced us all to realize that, just like there are different learning styles, there are different operating styles."

Having practiced being more trusting of others' work styles as a member of his cohort, Chris began to implement this practice at his firm. "The experience challenged me to evaluate how I can work with my staff more effectively. Today, I look at people more individually, assess their strengths, and encourage them to work in the style that plays to their strengths. It's helped employee morale and productivity. Had I not experienced its effectiveness firsthand in my learning team, it's unlikely I would have had the courage to change my behavior at the office."

Peer Accountability Is a Powerful Force

Peer accountability has reigned supreme ever since we were kids in school. Teachers who understood it wielded it as a carrot and a stick. They shined a light on the good students so that others would follow, and they punished the bad behavior of individuals by keeping the entire class after school. Both could be wickedly effective. In business, admitting to your colleagues that you failed them is often the toughest admission of all. The respect of your colleagues is your greatest currency, and it's strengthened when you are regarded as someone who does what he says he will do.

Bob Duncan offered this story about how a *culture of accountability* manifests in his group:

> One day a member of my group who was in his middle thirties at the time arrived at our meeting at 8:00 a.m. He looked terrible. I said to him, "You look exhausted. What's up?" He said, "Bob, you won't believe it. Last month, I put an issue on the table that you guys were so effective in helping me process. And then last night, I realized I had not worked on what I said I would work on. I didn't want to miss the meeting today, but I also didn't want to come unprepared so I stayed up half the night doing the things I promised to meet my commitment to the group."

The culture of accountability that exists in good peer advisory groups makes everybody better. Bob's group member would not allow himself to show up unprepared. He believed that doing so would have been an affront to the members who so generously invested their time helping him with his issue. CEOs tend to hold one another accountable because they care about one another. We've dedicated a full chapter (chapter 8) to accountability because it is such a powerful force for good in both optimizer and accelerator groups.

SHARED BELIEFS

Neither business nor life has to be a zero-sum game. There's such a thing as a win–win, and the whole can be greater than the sum of its parts. Finding peers who share these beliefs and sensibilities results in a group capable of engaging in open and honest exchange, creating a confidential and safe environment for sharing both business and personal issues, and for holding one another accountable for the actions and the outcomes expressed by individual members. If you have what it takes to do this, you are on your way to realizing peer advantage.

SHARED GOALS

While understanding shared beliefs can help you know what to expect from a group experience, as well as what the group will expect from you, starting a group or choosing to join one involves finding people who are dedicated to achieving the same goal—whether that's a collective goal (to optimize) or an individual goal (to accelerate). You don't need to read a book about peer advisory groups to know that if you want to run marathons you should surround yourself with people who are also committed to that goal. That said, individuals seeking to run a marathon in under three hours have different requirements and expectations than those who hope to complete it in four hours or more. A train program for first-time runners may involve running four days a v for eighteen weeks and maxing out at thirty-five miles per week. under-three-hour plan may involve running five or six days a week for eighteen weeks, and peaking at more than fifty miles a week for multiple weeks. Of course, it's not just about running longer, but training faster. In addition to finding a group that shares your goal, it also helps if you select one that's operating at the right speed.

To apply this metaphor to business, groups made up of CEOs leading start-ups, small businesses, midsized companies, and large corporations are all having robust conversations. They're just having different conversations. Jim Alampi, author of *Great to Excellent,* refers to the various levels as *barriers.*[4] These are not barriers that are obstructions but barriers that need to be acknowledged. For example, in his 2013 book, Alampi said that 96 percent of the companies filing tax returns in the United States had fewer than ten employees. Addressing the small to midsized sector, he identified barriers in terms of how the requirements of running a business change when you move from a small company to a midsized organization on to a large corporation with thousands of employees.

If you're an entrepreneur or small business, you might explore groups run by Entrepreneurs' Organization (EO), Renaissance Executive Forums or The Alternative Board (TAB). If you lead a small to midsized company, check into the offerings at Vistage and Young Presidents' Organization (YPO), as there are a number of CEOs who are members of both. If you lead a Fortune 1000 company, consider looking at World 50 or CCI. We select these particular organizations only to make a point about seeking the right level for you. There are many other choices out there, including starting your own group. We encourage you to explore the option that's best for you.

HOW WILL YOU KNOW IF YOU'RE IN THE RIGHT GROUP?

Your group will let you know if it's the right one. By their very nature, CEO peer advisory groups provide honest and direct feedback. If you are at all apprehensive about your interactions with your peers, chances are they have the same concerns about you. Typically, and we've heard this from many leaders of CEO peer advisory groups, leaders will do a ninety-day check with the group. They'll ask questions to learn the value you believe you're receiving from the group and give you feedback on your participation. In most cases, these ninety-day checks go quite well, as a new member typically comes to the group with an understanding of the shared values. Of course, as in any healthy relationship, good communication is the glue that holds the group together.

A FEW WORDS ON GIVING AND RECEIVING

Ask most employees if they're giving more to their organizations than they are getting in return, and they'll respond with an answer such as, "Absolutely. I'm working eighty-hour weeks and helping the firm realize record topline sales." They hear the question as if they're being asked to justify the company's investment in them and then, unabashedly, if not defensively, they avow that the company is getting far more than it's paying for. From an employee's perspective, this is an excellent answer to the question. However, the boss, who is thinking about an employee's potential for advancement and long-term prospects, often views this answer through a different lens.

Pepperdine University professor Vance Caesar once shared a story from a time early in his business career when his boss asked him if he was giving more to the company than he was getting in return. He, too, offered an unequivocal response, stating that he was giving far more than he was receiving. Vance's supervisor, instead of beaming with appreciation, got angry. Vance was at a loss. He thought, "What did I say that was so wrong?" Later in the week, his supervisor posed the question again. Vance offered the same reply and received an even more enraged reaction. Vance was told to think about it over the weekend and that if he didn't have a better answer by Monday morning, he should be prepared to clean out his desk.

Totally perplexed and extremely worried about Monday's meeting, Vance called one of his mentors to explain the situation. His mentor replied, "It's highly unlikely you are giving more than you are getting." As Vance began to defend his position, the mentor stopped him and asked, "Are you developing as a leader? Are you learning? Are you building relationships that will help you grow?" He continued to ask questions and eventually helped Vance see the dozens of benefits he was receiving from his employer beyond salary and bonus. Vance now realized what his supervisor was trying to tell him.

On Monday morning, Vance met with his supervisor, who was holding a resignation letter ready for signature. When asked the question a third time, Vance answered, "No, I'm getting more than I'm giving." "Why?" the supervisor asked. Vance then explained all the ways he benefited from being an employee. Vance's newfound, expanded view of what he was receiving from the organization was precisely what the supervisor was waiting to hear. He explained that Vance was being groomed for a leadership position in the company and that when employees believe they are giving more than they are getting, it's only matter of time before the seeds of resentment begin to grow and take over, forever damaging the employee's perspective of the relationship with the company. Vance's supervisor kept the resignation letter in his desk drawer, telling him that if he ever slipped in this regard, he would be asked to sign that letter.

This perspective on giving and receiving is essential if you want to avail yourself of the benefits of peer advantage. If you're considering whether a CEO peer advisory group is right for you, ask yourself if you believe in the true meaning of the phrase "It's better to give than to receive." It doesn't mean you should give more than you receive; it means giving is receiving in more ways than one. In the context of a

CEO peer advisory group, if you are prepared to give 100 percent of yourself to the group, you'll receive a six- to eight- to sixteenfold ROI from your colleagues (depending on the number of members), each of whom will be giving 100 percent to you.

SUMMARY

We covered what it means to give and receive, along with the shared beliefs that are essential to any good CEO peer advisory group:

1. A peer group is smarter than any one individual.
2. Leaders benefit from insightful questions and the impartial advice of their peers.
3. People prefer to implement their own solutions, rather than be told what to do and how to do it.
4. Success is the most effective means for driving positive behavioral change.
5. Leaders, regardless of industry sector, share common aspirations and challenges.
6. Leaders benefit from learning about industry practices not common to their own business.
7. Peer accountability is a powerful force.

The value of your group is negotiated between you and your group members, based on a simple formula: the more you give, the more you receive. Next, we'll cover the second of five factors essential to achieving peer advantage: a safe environment.

5

Create a Safe Environment

Greg Fricks and his brother Brad developed a ten-year succession plan to buy out their father at their family-owned high-performance concrete flooring business. The problem was that, when the time came to transfer ownership, their dad wasn't ready to hand over the reins. Despite the fact that the brothers paid the ten-year buyout agreement in five years, the father continued to draw a salary and benefits and used his influence in a manner that was adversely affecting business operations. Greg and his brother, having been brought up to respect their elders, could not find a way to confront their father. The father would routinely pit one brother against the other and use his emotional ties to get his way. This dynamic placed a strain on the business and on the family.

This was a very sensitive family issue, and Greg needed a safe environment where he could be open about his feelings, free from being judged by his fellow members, and be assured that anything that was said in the room, stayed in the room. This chapter discusses the necessity of having a confidential, trusting, and objective environment in which to solve challenging issues and create shared learning.

Imagine how deeply personal and important this subject was to Greg and Brad, to the survival of the business, and to the preservation of the extended family. The level of trust involved for this kind of dialogue requires an environment in which the individual participants can be totally vulnerable yet know they are completely safe. If you think about it, environments that afford complete safety are rare. For many of us, they may be nonexistent.

For Greg, the safe environment allowed him to receive the kind of support and encouragement from his group that helped him and his brother confront their father. When they did, their father was livid. A week later, however, he acknowledged that Greg and Brad were right, and that he was simply afraid to let go. The father stepped away from the business as promised, which not only eased family tensions that had been building for years but enabled the company to prosper—sales nearly tripled over the next twenty-four months.

FIGHTING OFF CAVEMAN MENTALITY

Bob Dabic, a former CEO who lives in Orange County, California, has been training leaders of CEO peer advisory groups for more than a decade and leading his own groups for longer than that. Here is Bob's account of one of the first things he says to candidates training to lead these groups:

> Here's all you need to do to have a high-performing group. It's pretty simple. All you need to do is overcome tens of thousands of years of human conditioning. Easy, right? It always gets a laugh. They get it. I say, all you have to do is overcome the cave day mentality. Of course back in the cave days, vulnerability equaled weakness, which all too often resulted in death. If you were vulnerable and a sabertooth tiger sensed you were vulnerable or weak, the sabertooth tiger was on your neck and it was all over. If you showed vulnerability and if rival tribe members sensed that you were vulnerable or weak and could take your possessions or food, they would do it. So, we come from a standpoint that it's not good to be vulnerable. Why would we ever put ourselves in that position? Why would we want to behave in a manner that makes us look weak?

Brené Brown, author of *Daring Greatly*, talks about the myths of vulnerability. One is that vulnerability is weakness. During her research for the book, Brown asked research participants to finish this sentence: "Vulnerability is _____." Sample responses included starting a business, having faith, and admitting being afraid of something. Brown says that vulnerability sounds like the truth and feels like courage.[1]

In a business setting, no one is going to die or risk starvation from appearing vulnerable. It's not about death, it's about the fear of being judged. It should be about being courageous and telling the truth. Unfortunately, too many people regard sharing a messy problem, not knowing the answer to a question, or demonstrating a lack of competence in a particular discipline as a sign of weakness, and they fear they will be judged or ridiculed in one form or another.

Bob Dabic said, "The challenge with working with members on being open and vulnerable is in showing them how they can challenge others in a way that doesn't communicate judgment. To the extent that feedback can be constructive or come from a neutral platform is essential to creating a safe environment." Members must understand that they can be vulnerable and that they will neither die nor be judged.

Beyond overcoming human conditioning and our fear of being judged, there's another layer at work here that makes creating a safe environment even more challenging. The truth is, there are very few, if any, places in our society where you are afforded the luxury of true safety. We live in a world where we are constantly being judged, where at every turn people are judging our actions. For CEOs, this is especially true. Letting your guard down is extremely difficult because it requires you to consider that this new environment—the peer advisory group setting—is different from anything else you've experienced in your life. That's a big leap. You may believe that when you join a peer advisory group, the members are asking you to trust first, and you will receive trust in return. The good news is that just the opposite is true. It's likely that during your first meeting someone will share a personal story, and you will quickly recognize that this is the first time that member has ever told it out loud. The group is way ahead of you. The water is fine.

GROUP NORMS

While new group members may understand intellectually that vulnerability equals strength, not weakness, and that being open and vulnerable with the group is essential to realizing true peer advantage, it's hard to know what the environment is really like or how you'll respond until you experience your first group meeting. Most leaders of a CEO peer advisory group engage in an orientation or onboarding process to help new members maximize their experience from the very first meeting, but before that, new members need to understand and commit to group norms.

At Vistage, CEO group leaders lean heavily on the company values of trust, caring, challenge, and growth to communicate group norms. When viewed as a list, each of the four values stands firmly on its own. If you look at the values from a linear perspective, you'll see they are sequential: trust is where it all starts. It's the bedrock of any relationship. After building trust, people can have faith in the sincerity and depth of other members' caring, which allows group members to challenge one another from a positive position and helps them foster personal and professional growth. The order of caring and challenge, and their position between trust and growth, creates a proverbial yin and yang relationship. These are not opposing forces so much as forces that rely on each other to be effective. Additionally, if you look at the values as a systems thinker, it's easy to see that the values form a reinforcing loop because growth breeds more trust—and the cycle continues.

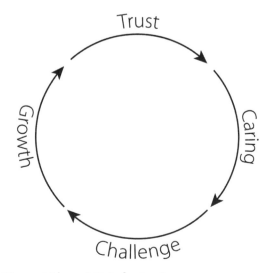

FIGURE 5.1   Vistage Values: A Reinforcing Loop

These values, which were established nearly sixty years ago, have stood the test of time. To sustain this cycle, members understand that all meetings are under the "Vegas Rule": what happens in the meeting stays in the meeting. Confidentiality is sacrosanct, but this essentially refers to what occurs outside the meeting. Inside the meeting, peer advisory group leaders emphasize being a learner rather than a judger. This is crucial for creating an environment in which members can be vulnerable and feel safe.

Fredricka Brecht, who leads CEO peer advisory groups in Texas, said, "People who come from a position of judgment have a hard time creating safety for others or for themselves." If you're a judger rather than a learner, it's unlikely you would ever feel comfortable being vulnerable in a group setting because all you can imagine is others mirroring your behavior. You would always feel you're being judged because that's the position you're coming from. As a learner, you feel safe to reveal your most inner thoughts and feelings because when you're learning, you know you're not going to be right all the time, so you can make mistakes and, by your example, give others the freedom to do so as well.

YPO provides a second example of communicating group norms, as group members are asked to sign a code of conduct every year. Unless you accept the code, you will not be invited to renew your membership.

- Act with integrity and uphold your reputation and that of YPO-WPO.
- Always respect member confidentiality.
- Respond to members within twenty-four hours.
- Do not solicit members unless invited to do so.

Sue Hesse of Hesse Partners works with YPO-WPO, Entrepreneurs' Organization, Lean In, and HBS forums all over the world. She shares a suggested forum mission as follows: "Our mission is to become better people/leaders by sharing our business, family and personal lives in an atmosphere of confidentiality, trust, respect and intimacy. We commit to ourselves and each other the time, resources and opportunity to achieve the personal, professional and spiritual growth we desire."[2]

Sue also stresses safety and confidentiality, and provides specific guidance to Hesse Partners' forum clients in this regard.

- ■ Confidentiality is the first among the critical principles of Forum success. Every member may be assured that nothing said in Forum will ever be repeated by another member outside the group.
- ■ Forum business is discussed outside the meeting only in private and only with other Forum members. However, a member may request a higher level of confidentiality beyond this norm. Nothing is discussed with outsiders, except with the permission of the information holder.
- ■ Confidentiality is absolute, in all ways and forever. A member who leaves the Forum is not free to discuss what was learned about other members while in Forum. New members to the Forum are not privileged to the history of former members of the group.
- ■ If a member believes he/she has been breached, the breached member will contact the breaching member (if known) to discuss the situation; the breached member will also contact the moderator, who will investigate the incident (as necessary). If it is verified that a breach has occurred, the breaching member will submit his/her resignation.
- ■ If a member realizes he/she has breached another member, the breaching member will contact the breached member to advise him/her of the incident and to apologize. The breaching member will then contact the moderator to submit his/her resignation.
- ■ All breaches or suspected breaches are Forum business and will be brought to the Forum for discussion and resolution. Because trust has been broken, most Forums will accept the member's resignation.
- ■ The law takes precedence over the pledge of confidentiality. If a member is subpoenaed by a court of law, that member must testify.[3]

In our research, we've found that the group norms we described in the Vistage and YPO examples are consistent with the way other CEO peer advisory groups operate. There's a consensus that confidentiality and safety are the keys to what makes these groups so powerful and effective. While being fully acquainted with group norms about safety and confidentiality is a good start, a dedicated onboarding or member orientation can be essential for exercising your vulnerability muscles.

THE VALUE OF ONBOARDING

During interviews we conducted with dozens of peer advisory group leaders, several of them shared best practices that revealed common themes regarding onboarding activities. Here is a composite overview of several of the ideas that capture how CEO peer advisory group leaders typically approach onboarding.

The first and most important step is to engage the member as an equal. When that happens, new members feel welcomed as an equal partner in the group experience, and understand that they are now part of a group that cares about their personal and professional growth. The new member is also introduced as a valuable contributor to the group by explaining the nature of the contribution, the perspective this new member can provide, and how it will strengthen the group as a whole. The flip side is that the new member receives written profiles of each member of the group before the first meeting. These profiles tend to offer more detail about the group members than what was shared with the new member prior to joining, providing the next level of background information about group members. At the first meeting a new member attends, every member will take a few minutes to talk about who he is, how long he's been in the group, and the biggest value he receives from being a member. Group members are also encouraged to reach out to the new member outside the meeting to build additional early rapport.

New members are often asked to share stories about their lives and identify any weaknesses they may have. The objective is to inspire questions and invite dialogue. By doing so, new members open up, and because of the preparation they received before the meeting, they're typically ready to share. This often involves challenging the members to prepare an issue they would like to bring to the group. We found that new members are typically eager to bring a range of issues to the group. These are not necessarily problems, as much as prospective opportunities they want to share or imminent decisions on which they'd like advice. As a result, they become quickly and rather seamlessly immersed in the group.

TO HAVE SAFETY, YOU HAVE TO BUILD TRUST

Jim Kouzes, coauthor of *The Leadership Challenge,* says that if you want to build trust, everyone needs to feel the same level of vulnerability. Jim told us, "One way to accomplish this is through self-disclosure." In a group setting among CEOs, you might start by asking them to talk about the highs and lows in their careers or their work lives. They can go back as far as they want into their childhoods, but they should talk to the group about both the high points and low points of their lives. This type of conversation gets people to open up and begin to understand the other members of the group, particularly when they talk about low points in their career and things that happened to them—whether it was getting fired from a job, losing a spouse, or another particularly difficult time at work or at home. When members talk about these low points from the past, others ask them questions about how they climbed out of it. What did they call upon within themselves to make that possible?

Discussion of the low points should be balanced by talk about high points—members can appreciate what others have accomplished and what's most meaningful to them. Group leaders should ask members to talk about what motivated them to achieve those peaks in their careers and in their personal lives. "Any type of exercise that gets people talking about their successes as well as their failures will help them become a more trusting group," Jim said.

Over time, Bob Dabic noted that creating an environment where it's safe to be vulnerable involves everyone taking turns being the lead bicyclist. "The lead bicyclist cuts through the wind and lets others draft behind. By the lead bicyclist, I mean, you bring a messy topic or issue before your group. It could be business, could be personal. The other members see that your willingness to be vulnerable provided you with value. They realize you were able to survive being vulnerable and not emotionally die or feel self-conscious or embarrassed. It provides, I believe, permission for the others then to take turns in the next meeting being the lead bicyclist, cutting through the wind with their vulnerable, messy topic."

VULNERABILITY REWARDED

For Scot Dietz, "head cheese" (yes, that's his real title) at 3 Blind Mice Window Coverings, business was going gangbusters. In 2006, the *San Diego Business Journal* recognized Scot's company as the second-fastest-growing company in the region. During that time, he joined a peer advisory group because, despite his success, he believed joining a group would expose him to people who had the experience to help him take his business to the next level. Then the recession hit, and it hit Scot's business hard. Instead of flying high and relying on his group to help grow his business, he needed his group to either help him save his company or file bankruptcy.

Scot said, "In 2006, we were growing, growing, growing. Then when the subprime market melted down and other dominoes began to fall, we suffered a 34 percent decrease in sales. The next year, we had a 34 percent decrease in sales. The year after that sales fell another 24 percent. We were hemorrhaging. We went from a $5.5 million company to $1.2 million company in a matter of three years."

At the time, Scot had to come up with about $8,000 a month to cover the lease on his space. He admitted to the group that he was drowning. Scot said:

> I'll never forget the day that I asked my fellow members if I should stay in business or file bankruptcy. Getting everyone's perspective on everything I needed to think about was enormously helpful, and their encouragement gave me the strength to press on. But in my case, it was even more than that. One of

my members went so far as to invite me to work out of space he and his wife had available free of charge for six months. They proposed to charge me $500 a month for the six months to follow, and normal market rate after that. Going from $8,000 monthly rent to zero allowed me to operate my business. Today, we're back stronger than ever.

Part of what gave me the courage to share my troubles with the group involved what my group leader refers to as *carefrontation*. He says it's where people are open and they confront one another from a place of caring. And they do so in a manner that preserves dignity and respect. That is the culture of our group, summed up in a single word. We are relentlessly *carefrontational*. My group was there for me for years, as I worked my way back. You can't go anywhere in the world and get that kind of support and feedback in such a manner that allows you to hear it.

SAFETY INSPIRES OPENNESS

As Scot was experiencing the toughest stretch of his career, he didn't shut down, he opened up. Each member has to be completely open—intellectually and emotionally. The group cannot be effective in advising a member if that member is only sharing part of the story. Issues don't just have sides, they have dimensions that extend beyond a factual understanding of what's going on. Lack of openness typically results in an incomplete understanding of the issue being discussed. The result is that the group comes up with the right solution to the wrong problem. Complete openness not only allows the group to understand what is going on but why it's going on. With this knowledge, the group helps the member identify the root cause of the issue being discussed.

THE DANGER OF MISSTEPS

Members make mistakes, and their mistakes can have a far-reaching impact—this is why the group and its leader try to avoid missteps at all cost. An example of a misstep is a member being openly disrespectful in response to comments from another member. The effect of this type of behavior may be that the member who is criticized is less likely to share in the future, but it can also serve as a warning to others in the group that they need to be on guard as well. If a misstep is not addressed immediately, a single act can hurt the group dynamic in the long term. Repeated acts of such disrespect to others would necessitate dismissal from the group, as no single member is more important than the collective. Our research revealed that such a dismissal is a rare occurrence.

A single misstep, however, doesn't have to poison the well. Jim Kouzes recalls this story about his colleague and coauthor Barry Posner:

> I remember my colleague, Barry Posner, was leading a workshop where he was getting people to do the "trust fall." In thirty years of doing this, neither Barry nor I have ever seen anyone get hurt. People tend to do their job and catch the person before they hit the ground. So one day, at the end of the workshop, one of the participants said, "Professor Posner, why don't you do the trust fall?" He said, "I've done it many times, so here's what I'll do. Instead of falling over, I'm going to lie on the ground underneath and I'm going to take a photograph of everyone catching one of you as he falls. So remember, you have to catch this person, like you've done before, because if you don't he will fall right on top of me." The group all agreed it was a great idea.
>
> So Barry got down on the ground, and aimed his camera up at the person who was standing on a stepladder about three or four feet off the ground. The participant fell over backward, but for some reason, even though they'd done this perfectly about twenty times during the course of the day, the team members didn't catch the faller, and that person landed right on Barry. You can imagine the impact. The faller wasn't injured, but Barry totally lost his breath for a few moments.
>
> The participants were shocked, and they began expressing their concerns saying, "Oh my god, Professor Posner, are you all right? Are you all right? Anything wrong with you? Are you okay? We're sorry." After catching his breath he said, "Yeah, I'm

fine. I'll be okay." (Later, Barry would learn that he had cracked a couple of ribs.) They turned to him and said, "Oh, I bet you're not going to do that ever again." He paused and thought for a moment and then he said, "Actually, I will. I think this has taught us all something very important. There are really just two rules when it comes to trust. Rule number one is: you have to keep working on trust and never take it for granted. Rule number two is: sometimes trust breaks down. So, see rule number one." Of course, that's true in all relationships: "Sometimes trust breaks down. When it does, see rule number one."

SUMMARY

Being vulnerable is liberating. When you're in an environment that affords you the freedom to share your innermost thoughts—when you can reveal to others that you are scared, concerned, or unsure about any situation in your life, personal or professional, without fear of being judged—and know that the group has your back, there's nothing quite like it. Before group members feel comfortable opening up, however, they need a safe environment inside the meeting and to see that all members have a healthy respect for confidentiality outside the meeting. Creating that environment is everyone's responsibility.

If you want to get the most out of your CEO peer advisory group, or any other relationship, for that matter, regard vulnerability not as a weakness but as a strength. It takes courage to be vulnerable. And, according to Brené Brown, "vulnerability is the birthplace of innovation, creativity and change."[4]

Next we'll cover the third of the five factors—the role of the group leader and why an effective leader is the lynchpin of peer advantage.

6

Utilize a Smart Guide

We struggled to come up with an all-encompassing, neutral term for the person who is charged with leading a CEO peer advisory group. Chair, chairperson, facilitator, and group leader were a few of the common names we considered. As we continued to explore the various models for group leadership, we discovered they came in many forms—from those guided by a professionally trained facilitator, who serves as the permanent leader of the CEO members, to member-led groups in which the member–leader may or may not receive formal training, to member-led groups in which leadership rotates among the members over time. Whatever the model, certain common denominators were consistent: all groups benefited from having a leader, and the traits an effective group leader needed to possess were largely the same. Leaders need to be good listeners, willing to help others, passionate about the role, and adept at fostering strong relationships among the members both inside and outside the group. They must be the stewards of the other four factors, making sure the right people are in the group and contributing in a positive way, maintaining a safe and confidential environment, fostering valuable interactions, and creating a culture of accountability. To do so, the leader needs to be smart and seek to guide the group rather than direct it, hence the term "smart guide."

The purpose of this chapter isn't to teach you how to be a smart guide; it's primarily designed to allow members and prospective group members to gain some insights into how these groups are run and why effective guidance is so crucial to maximizing the potential of the group.

A SMART GUIDE IN ACTION

Leon shares this story: The very first peer group meeting I attended was Norma Rosenberg's group in New York City. Norma's peer group had about fifteen CEO members. One of the members that day, the owner of a supply business, brought an issue to the group. Bob co-owned the business with his older brother, Paul. They had recently discovered a serious inventory issue that could adversely affect their largest customer and put the entire relationship at risk. The customer was not yet aware of the issue. If not resolved, there would be an enormous financial burden on their business. Bob met with his brother who recommended that they finance a solution that would also enable them to expand the business with better systems.

Bob brought a full set of financial projections, business plan, balance sheet, etc., to review with the group. Norma watched as Bob shared the financial and business plan. When he mentioned a discussion he had with his brother, Norma quietly leaned in and asked Bob to share a little more detail about that conversation. About five minutes later, when Bob referred to a disagreement he and his brother had over the business plan, Norma again suggested that he share more about that interaction.

Norma had the benefit of meeting with Bob prior to the group meeting, which she typically did every month for two hours. During one of those one-to-one meetings, she surmised that Bob was struggling with a deeper issue—the brothers clearly had fundamentally different views on how the business should be run. To further complicate matters, Bob had never discussed these concerns with Paul. Norma could easily have suggested to Bob that he confront his brother and talk about their issues. She also knew that she had a much more powerful resource at her disposal—Bob's peer group.

By gently guiding the conversation at Bob's group meeting, Norma knew that she would accomplish several things that would lead to a much better outcome for Bob. The fact that his peers recognized the obvious eight-hundred-pound gorilla in the room would speak volumes. Bob would not be able to avoid confronting the *real* issue, and hearing that message from his peers, who were motivated by nothing other than helping Bob, would be much more impactful. More importantly, the group would hold Bob accountable for following up on his commitment, and Bob, in turn, would feel a real sense of accountability to his group. He would *own* the issue.

I watched in awe as Norma skillfully prompted Bob to share the whole story and expertly guided the group through a tried and proven process that flushed out the real angst that Bob was feeling (*or the real fear Bob was avoiding*). The questions they asked Bob allowed his mind to open up and hear things in a way he wouldn't have considered otherwise.

Bob benefited immensely from the guidance and insights of fifteen experienced CEOs reviewing his business plan. Yet that benefit paled in comparison to the impact of resolving the fundamental issue he had with his brother.

WHAT DOES GREAT PEER ADVISORY GROUP LEADERSHIP LOOK LIKE?

The challenge for group leaders is straightforward, but not easy. How can you help your members be at their best both inside and outside the group meeting, professionally and personally? Having a passion for the work is certainly at the top of the list, and to that end we came to know Pat Hyndman as a true exemplar. Pat's success as a leader of CEO and executive peer advisory groups was rooted in his passion for the work, boundless energy, and wealth of experience. Pat died in 2013 at age ninety-eight, still actively leading his groups. Many of Pat's group members had been with him for more than a decade, so the loss was a difficult one. To this day, the members of Pat's group frequently recall his ability to harness individual experiences and the group's collective wisdom for everyone's benefit. His members grew and so did their companies. They have Pat to thank for it.

Interestingly enough, Pat didn't start leading peer advisory groups until age seventy-three. What's more remarkable, however, is that he enjoyed doing so for nearly twenty-five years. Pat regarded the time he invested with his members as the most meaningful work of his life, largely because he saw the big picture. He wasn't just helping a CEO make more money or build a larger company, he had a hand in creating jobs, helping families buy homes, providing people with the capacity to give time and money to not-for-profits in their communities, and making a real difference in people's lives that extended far beyond a company payroll.

Prior to embarking on this work, Pat had a career rich with leadership roles in business, education, philanthropy, and cultural affairs throughout California. A graduate of the University of California, Berkeley, he founded the PHD Corporation, a national truck, car, and equipment leasing company, in 1953. He served as its chief executive officer until the firm's sale to Leaseway Transportation Corporation twenty-five years later. In addition to his business accomplishments over the years, Pat served for more than two decades on the San Diego County Board of Education. He played an active role in establishing the University of California, San Diego campus and is regarded among its founders. All of these experiences, among many others, contributed in one way or another to Pat Hyndman's legacy as a group leader, husband, and father.

Even in his late nineties, Pat remained current on technology and business practices. He had the presence and strength of voice of someone thirty years his junior and was imbued with a brand of wisdom drawn from nearly a century's worth of rich experiences. Over the decades during which he led peer advisory groups, Pat's members benefited from his guiding hand and infectious enthusiasm for learning. Always curious, Pat often said, "People don't grow old, they become old when they stop growing." As we continue this chapter on the value of a peer advisory group being led by a "smart guide," we do so with Pat Hyndman in mind.

Filling Pat's shoes may be a tall order, but if your smart guide possesses the desire, passion, skills, brain, heart, and stomach to handle the responsibility that comes with guiding your group, even if just for one meeting, then you'll all be the big winners.

SERVANT LEADERSHIP

Servant leadership was a common theme among those we interviewed about the role of the smart guide. Servant leadership is a term coined by Robert Greenleaf in 1970 in his essay "The Servant Leader." A number of years ago, Leo interviewed Kent M. Keith, who served as the CEO (2007–12) of what is now called the Robert K. Greenleaf Center. In discussing how servant leadership came about, Kent said that Robert Greenleaf worked for AT&T for thirty-eight years before retiring in 1964. Toward the end of his career, Greenleaf was director of management research, training senior leaders and managers for the company. After retiring, he concluded that the power culture of leadership he had seen at AT&T didn't work very well.[1] In the early 1990s, Sue Cartwright and Cary Cooper defined these power cultures by their tendencies toward centralized decision making and reward and punishment structures tied to personal loyalties, which often resulted in poor morale among employees who felt disempowered.[2]

Greenleaf saw a better way—servant leadership. In this leadership model, employees weren't there to make the leader successful, rather the leader was there to provide the resources and guidance to make employees successful. As you can imagine, this turned the traditional model of leadership on its head. Greenleaf's essay launched the modern-day servant leadership movement.

Servant leaders identify and meet the needs of others. Keith defined a servant leader this way:

It begins with the natural feeling that one wants to serve, to serve first. Then conscious choice brings one to aspire to lead. That person is sharply different from one who is leader first, perhaps because of the need to assuage an unusual power drive or to acquire material possessions...

The difference manifests itself in the care taken by the servant-first to make sure that other people's highest priority needs are being served. The best test, and difficult to administer, is: Do those served grow as persons? Do they, while being served, become healthier, wiser, freer, more autonomous, more likely themselves to become servants?[3]

Experts understand the importance of servant leadership. The list of luminaries who have spoken at Greenleaf Center conferences over the years reads like a *Who's Who* of leadership. They include Warren Bennis,

Ken Blanchard, Stephen Covey, Max De Pree, Joseph Jaworski, Jim Kouzes, Peter Senge, and Margaret Wheatley—all of whom voiced their support for the concept of servant leadership. Keith noted that other experts describe servant leaders without using that label: "Peter Drucker's 'effective executive' is a servant leader, as is Jim Collins's 'Level 5' leader."

According to Kent, examples of servant leaders include George Washington, Abraham Lincoln, Harriet Tubman, Susan B. Anthony, Albert Schweitzer, Mahatma Gandhi, Mother Teresa, Cesar Chavez, and Martin Luther King, Jr. "Most servant leaders are only known within their organizations and communities. They are not trying to be famous, they are trying to make a difference—and they do," Kent said.

BEING A GOOD LISTENER

The specific principles and practices of servant leadership are interwoven with what we learned were important traits for leading a peer advisory group. Topping the list is the need to be a good listener. You not only have to be able to listen, you also have to be able to hear what's being said and recognize what's not being said. The art of listening is probably one of the more powerful pieces of leadership. Kent noted that comprehensive listening is essential for the servant leader because if you don't know what someone's true needs are, you'll never be able to meet those needs.

GREAT QUESTIONS AND FIERCE CONVERSATIONS

If you want to get to the heart of someone's needs, you need to do more than just listen, of course. You have to know how to ask really good questions. Better yet, many of the best peer advisory group leaders are schooled in the art of what author Susan Scott calls "fierce conversations," also the title of her 2002 best-selling book. Scott describes the seven steps of fierce conversations as: (1) determining the most pressing issue, (2) clarifying the issue, (3) reviewing the current impact, (4) deciding what will happen if nothing changes, (5) determining one's personal contribution, (6) describing the ideal outcomes, and (7) committing to action. How to ask good questions will be covered in greater detail in chapter 7, but these skills stand at the center of being a good servant leader and an effective smart guide.

REACHING YOUR OWN CONCLUSIONS

The best peer group leaders think of themselves as coaches rather than consultants. Consultants are problem solvers who recommend solutions for you, while smart guides help you reach your own conclusions and, working with the group, develop your own solutions. They guide you by helping you help yourself. There's a whole lot of science to support the idea that solutions, directions, plans, goals, ideas, etc., are more successful if the people implementing them arrive at the solution themselves.

For example, you've probably known people who are smokers. You can ask them to quit, their doctor can tell them to quit, and a mountain of evidence that smoking is hazardous to their health can rise before them—they still don't quit. Then one day, because they receive adverse medical news about their own health or suffer some sort of episode, they decide it's time to quit smoking. Without some sense of urgency and the belief that they're making and owning the decision, the odds of them actually quitting are low. Is that true for everyone? Of course not, but it's true for a lot of us. Those who have a hand in creating the solution tend to follow through more often.

RELATIONSHIP BUILDING

The best smart guides also have a wonderful ability to help group members build relationships that transcend the meeting and, in some instances, even the need for the leader. Bob Duncan described these kinds of groups as "armed and dangerous" in chapter 4. Saundra Johnson, who led CEO peer advisory groups in the Las Vegas area for a number of years, offered this example of how a leader can encourage a group to work together on its own:

A member called me about three days after the meeting and said, "Look, something critical has come up with my business, very critical." Since the group just had its meeting a few days earlier, it was going to be almost a month before everyone got back together and the member couldn't wait. "I need their help." So I asked him what he would like to do. "Well, I know today's Friday but tomorrow I would love to get together in the morning with the members that I know have the knowledge and experience to really help with this." He then started rattling off a bunch of names. He said, "Jim, Joe, Sam, David, and Bob for starters." He then asked, "Can you call those people and see if they can meet with me?" I told him yes, but that I thought he should reach out to them, which he did. Now, that may sound simple, but it's important that I'm not always at the hub of the member-to-member interaction. I didn't even have to go to the meeting. The point being that now this truly was a peer group that not only was valuable beyond me as the leader, but sustainable beyond me because it was about their relationships with each other.

A PASSION FOR THE WORK

A wonderful story about the passion that's palpable in leaders who love to do this work comes from Doug Baker, who coauthored *True North Groups* with Bill George in 2011. For background, a True North Group is a small group of people with whom we can have in-depth discussions and share intimately about the most important things in our lives—our happiness and sadness, our hopes and fears, our beliefs and convictions.[4] These self-organized, member-led groups are typically made up of no more than six to eight members.

Doug, who has been leading and working with others in small groups for decades, talked about one of his first group experiences. The group was led by a college professor who, during Doug's years as an undergraduate student, inspired the way Doug leads and engages group members even today:

One of my favorite professors in college was a guy who taught economics. The course I took from him was for graduate students, and even though I was still an undergrad, he let me in anyway. It was the most fun and best learning experience I ever had, largely because of the way he worked with us. The students were largely Korean War vets, so all these guys were older. I was the youngest student there by five years. We met at a beer garden twice a week for three hours. It was a bull session. It was the sage professor bringing up ideas and talking and giving his perspective and asking ours—sparking a dynamic and healthy back-and-forth discussion. I took three courses from this guy simply because his passion was infectious, and I always learned so much—not just from him but from everyone.

THE GROUP LEADERSHIP STRUCTURE

Imagine for a moment you are charged with leading a peer advisory group of CEOs. You might have a tendency to think of yourself as a leader in terms of being at the center or standing in the front of the room with all eyes focused on you.

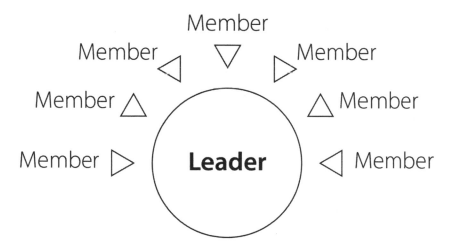

FIGURE 6.1   A Stage Three CEO Peer Advisory Group

Interestingly enough, the peer group leaders we talked to said that you can't lead a peer advisory group in that way—at least not for very long. The model shown here fails to recognize the group as an entity, nor does it account for the need for members to bond with one another. If you recall our reference to Dave Logan's work from the book *Tribal Leadership*, you'll remember that 50 percent of companies operate with the Stage Three culture of "I'm great, you're not." The model shows you what Stage Three looks like. All members are focused squarely on the leader, waiting to hear whatever infinite wisdom comes their way. There is no group or team per se, just a collection of relationships that form dyads directly between the leader and the member.

The smart guide's job, as Duncan and Johnson described earlier, is to create camaraderie among the members so that they depend on one another as much as, or more than, they do the leader.

TRIADS

The leader should neither sit at the head of the class nor be a constant center of attention—the servant leader (smart guide) is part of the group, not someone who stands apart from it.

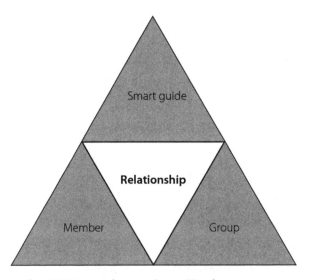

FIGURE 6.2   The CEO Peer Advisory Group Triad

Think of the group as a triad, with the smart guide, an individual member, and the group at the three corners, holding the relationship in the middle. According to Logan's model, Stage Four and Stage Five cultures tend to work in triads rather than dyads. Triads become essential for effective communication. For example, if a member and the group are involved in a complex conversation, the smart guide sees to it that the member and the group fully understand each other. If the member happens to misunderstand what the group is saying, the smart guide will step in and clarify. The smart guide "has the back" of the relationship, as Logan likes to say. If the smart guide and the group find themselves in a similar situation, an individual member might spot the misunderstanding and offer clarification. When the smart guide, the individual member, and the group accept responsibility for holding up their part of the relationship, the relationship has greater potential for stability and growth.

Several smart guides told us that triads are essential not only for group stability but group sustainability. If the smart guide operates on a hub-and-spoke model, in which everything goes through the leader, it's unlikely the group would stay together for very long. Saundra Johnson said, "I'm not, and I would say that nobody is, smart enough to have every answer to every question. My value will run its course if everything comes through me. If we're all working together, with the infinite knowledge that exists in the room, the group sustains itself."

The best smart guides lead their groups with a keen eye toward stability and sustainability. Here are a few other ways they do it.

REINFORCE GROUP NORMS

We covered the importance of establishing group norms in chapter 5, but it would be a mistake for the smart guide to take established norms for granted. They require constant nurturing. Confidentiality is sacrosanct and the safety of the environment is a cultural imperative. Leading a group successfully involves a measure of assertiveness, particularly with these matters; the leader can't be wishy-washy. The smart guide has to lead the group and preserve the norms that help it function effectively. The group has to operate well if it is ever going to create value for the individual members.

For the smart guide, creating value involves leading conversations that establish a level playing field for the group and remove possibilities for ambiguity about group norms. For example, a smart guide may ask group members to offer their definitions of words such as "accountability," "confidentiality," or "safety" to achieve shared meaning. Next, the smart guide may ask, "How important is safety to the group experience?" and "What would it mean to the group if someone's emotional or intellectual safety was compromised?" These questions frequently lead to rich conversations about the value of group norms, which quite often find their way back to the CEOs' organizations. Developing a shared understanding of expectations and responsibilities is an essential part of the smart guide's responsibility.

CREATING AN ATMOSPHERE FOR LEARNING

Hay Group's Cecelia Wooden said that if you really want people to learn and if you want to expose them to new ideas that will stick, you need to take them out of their comfort zones: "Adults enjoy their equilibrium; they like being comfortable. I would hope that any smart guide would make group members feel uncomfortable, because that's when adults learn. By placing individuals into disequilibrium, they also begin the process of returning to equilibrium. When this happens, they tend to reorganize the file cabinets in their mind and create new file cabinets. They assimilate the information. Then they accommodate it and ultimately learn something they never would have expected."

This kind of atmosphere is important, particularly for CEOs, who are rarely taken out of their comfort zones back at their organizations. Cecelia added, "Striving for peer advantage is nothing short of an act of courage. For a CEO to say, 'I want to have my assumptions examined. I want to have the way in which I look at things seen through other lenses, so that I might have greater clarity and a broader view.' That's a big deal."

For the member, this willingness to move out of her comfort zone takes self-assuredness, self-awareness, and dedication to lifelong learning.

For the smart guide, it requires a fearless commitment to creating a learning environment that works for high-powered individuals. Chapter 7 will explore more thoroughly how this is achieved in the group meeting.

INJECTING FUN AND CREATIVITY

It can't be just about rules, as Norma Rosenberg stated earlier in the chapter; trying new things is essential to the vitality of the group experience. Norma said, "I call my group the High-Fliers because they're movers and shakers and they have gotten restless and bored with some of the traditions that we had for years. We are experimenting. We're being very creative. I'm listening to them. We're working on ideas that they have come up with, and they're responding really well to that."

Group meetings can be serious, as members dig deep to talk about weighty issues and tough challenges. The smart guides we interviewed suggested that somewhere in the day, it's essential to inject a little fun, a little levity.

Saundra Johnson said that, at first blush, you might think that business leaders, especially CEOs, wouldn't appreciate all this elementary stuff in the room, but that's really not the case. This is their time out of the office to work on their business and have a little fun, too. "For my meetings, I created a wall space, and all the group members knew that when they came across a Google alert, newspaper article, or whatever good news that involved one of the members, they would bring it with them to the meeting and hang it on the wall. Then we would celebrate the news together. It's simple but the members loved it because how many times do leaders really get an opportunity to celebrate something that's a big deal for them? We celebrated personal milestones as well, including birthdays or family weddings. It brought everyone closer together."

SUMMARY

Whether a peer group's smart guide is a highly trained professional facilitator or a member whose turn has come up to lead the next meeting, that person's responsibility is the same. True smart guides lead with the guiding hand of a servant leader; they listen, ask good questions, build camaraderie, consider themselves coaches rather than consultants, and wear their passion for the role on their sleeves. The triad structure reinforces the idea that the smart guide is part of the group, and that everyone has a role in having the back of the relationship. Solid smart guides reinforce group norms, create an atmosphere for learning, and have some fun while they're at it. It's precisely the way Pat Hyndman did it for a quarter century, and his legacy lives in the hearts and successes of his members.

In chapter 7, armed with the right group of peers, a safe and confidential environment, and excellent guidance, we'll explore what's behind the power of these groups and how peer advantage becomes possible.

7

Foster Valuable Interaction

In chapter 5, we discussed two examples of peer group members who were struggling with sensitive situations and approached their groups with the understanding that the environment was safe and that anything they shared would be held in the highest confidence. Greg Fricks approached his CEO group about the troubles he and his brother Brad were having with their father. Scot Dietz confided in his group that his once fast-growing company was in deep trouble in the wake of the recession. Honest conversations about difficult subjects require that the participants feel safe being open and transparent. They also require another crucial element: participants must believe that sharing their story will result in a positive outcome. If they don't, no matter how safe or confidential the setting may be, they're not likely to share their issue with the group.

Sometimes opening up to others through dialogue, with no expectation of reaching a decision of any kind, is personally beneficial. In these cases, people are not looking for a fix; they just want to be heard. For them, that's the positive outcome.

For those who want a fresh perspective and guidance that can help them make a decision, particularly about a complex issue, a loosely constructed conversation won't cut it. While safety and confidentiality provide the member with much-needed emotional comfort, a well-defined, proven process with specific rules of engagement is essential for fostering the sense of efficacy required to bring serious matters to a group of peers. In this chapter, we'll look at processes that drive the kind of valuable interaction necessary for achieving peer advantage.

DEFINING VALUABLE INTERACTION

For the purposes of this book, consider valuable interaction in terms of a conversation where all the participants are engaged. They understand precisely what's being talked about and are prepared to ask insightful questions that inspire focus and clarity for all the participants. Jeannette Hobson, who has been leading groups in the Newark, New Jersey, area for more than twenty years, described it this way: "It's where everybody's involved—not only in terms of their thoughts and experience, but also when it comes to empathy and imagining what someone's emotional reaction would be before they give advice. They want to be able to take that reaction and pose a comment or a question that moves the conversation forward. It's when everyone in the room learns something of value because they've been so involved in the conversation."

SKILLED DISCUSSION

In 1998, Robert Garmston and Bruce Wellman defined the concept of *skilled discussion* as a way of talking that leads to decisions. Generally speaking, a skilled discussion is designed to fully examine a situation and separate good ideas from bad ones in the hope that the best ideas or solutions will rise to the top. A discussion lacking a process or discipline can easily devolve, so members end up simply sharing information, tossing out ideas, and selling those ideas. In a free-flowing discussion, it's not uncommon for the group to reach decisions that are either based on incomplete information or are influenced in a particular direction by an individual in the room who has a strong personality. In these instances, the nod goes to the best advocates, not necessarily to the strongest ideas. As Garmston and Wellman note, "Skilled discussions are infused with rigorous critical thinking, mutual respect, weighing of options, and decision making that serves the groups' vision, values, and goals."[1]

These rich, skilled discussions don't happen by accident. To start, we'll look at processes that will help you *optimize*, to take what you do really well and become great. We'll revisit the Blue Angels' post-flight debrief, and look at it from a process perspective. We'll cover the informal and formal after-actions conducted by the Navy Seals, and we'll examine a process that business leaders can use in their quest to *accelerate*. These frameworks for creating skilled discussion are used by CEO peer groups throughout the world.

BLUE ANGELS POST-FLIGHT DEBRIEF

By conducting a post-flight debrief in which everyone is an equal, the Blue Angels create a safe environment for honest conversation. During the debrief, rank, age, and experience are nonfactors, as each member of the team is encouraged to be as candid as possible in evaluating the flight. People's lives depend on it. In addition, a debrief *process* guides the discussion. It's this process that makes skilled discussion possible.

As we discussed, the pilots each take a turn talking about what they did well and identifying specific mistakes they may have made during the flight. They refer to these mistakes as safeties, which are safety problems or violations. Each pilot not only identifies his safeties, but also commits to the squadron that the errors will be fixed next time. The pilot concludes his remarks by saying, "Glad to be here." This tradition refers to the gratitude each pilot feels for membership in the Blue Angels—these pilots know that others are assigned to the Mediterranean Sea or the Persian Gulf, and because those pilots put themselves in harm's way, they make flying with the Blue Angels a possibility for others. It's the Blue Angels' way of recognizing the service of fellow pilots.

After each pilot takes his turn, he receives critiques from two members of the team who are assigned specifically to observe and assess the flight from the ground and share their perspective. Reviewing video of the flight, they watch and rewatch specific maneuvers to get a complete picture of the performance and identify how it can be better next time. Other members of the team offer their observations about nonflight aspects of the performance, which, as we stated in chapter 3, include everything from the pilot's salute to his march to and from the aircraft. The debriefing process, while simple, ensures that the squadron covers every detail of every aspect of the performance.

Former Blue Angels pilot John Foley, who today works with companies on continuous improvement, uses principles he learned during his time as a member of the squadron. Foley said that what separates the Blue Angels from other great teams is the unique combination of attitude, habits, and worldview. Foley briefly summarized the difference this way:

> The Blue Angels share a *mind-set*, a special way of looking at the world and seeing the potential for success that is often hidden behind the obstacles and difficulties of daily life.
>
> The Blue Angels create a *culture of excellence* that surrounds, supports, and nourishes them.
>
> The Blue Angels *transcend expectations*; they continually improve, innovate, and seek higher levels of performance.[2]

Foley said that the biggest excuse company leaders make for not debriefing is that it takes too much time. He believes, however, that if debriefing becomes a habit, it actually saves time because you don't have people making the same mistakes over and over again.

NAVY SEALS' AFTER-ACTION REVIEWS

Former Navy Seal Brandon Andrews today travels the country sharing the principles and practices of the Navy Seals with CEOs and business leaders. When Leon and Brandon first met, Brandon shared that, for the Navy Seals, there are two kinds of what he calls "after actions," informal and formal. Informal reviews are used largely to critique individual training runs, while a formal after-action review is reserved for larger training exercises or important missions. These more elaborate reviews are conducted in front of the larger leadership team and documented for the learning benefit of future platoons.

The informal review is structured around three basic questions: What went well? What didn't go well? What's going to be done to get it fixed for the next time? Brandon said, "For us, after-actions are happening constantly with every single thing that we do. For example, we do house runs in training. We do thousands of these. We might do forty to fifty runs in a day, and we would meet after every run. We simply bring the team together real quick and while there are no formal or informal write-ups, they are essential for continuous improvement."

In leading informal reviews, the leader must facilitate a conversation that allows everything to surface as the team works to answer the three questions. Typically, the leader accomplishes this by example. The leader often prefaces the review by reiterating that the mission and team come first, and he lives that statement by being the first to critique himself. He essentially humbles himself in front of the men, to make everyone feel more comfortable and to emphasize that nothing should be left unsaid. Even in these rather informal reviews, safety and process are essential. Brandon said, "Our mistakes are filled with grit and blood so it's a big deal, but in business it could mean the difference between millions of dollars if someone doesn't say, 'Hey guys, I dropped the ball on this. I screwed this up. Ultimately, it worked out for us, but let's all take note of it so no one else makes that mistake, and we don't have to worry about that ever again.'"

When it comes to the formal after-action review, the leader who has the most situational awareness of the mission or situation runs the session. That person will create a detailed, often chronological, agenda based on the specific nature of the training exercise or mission. It will often include PowerPoint slides and other training aids. These reviews are conducted very formally because the larger leadership is in the room, and the session is documented for future reference.

Brandon said:

For us, we'd all come in after the mission, and we would meet and present in front of our Officer in Charge (OIC) and our Chief. A PowerPoint and a write-up would then be sent up chain of command. That would go into a system where anyone in the entire military can read the account of our mission. The point of that is, if you're going into operate in the northern part of Afghanistan to go after Taliban, it might behoove you to read an after action of operations that have happened in that exact town. This way you can learn from the mistakes and successes that the Navy Seals, Green Berets, or anyone else has had.

This process can be extremely beneficial for leaders of companies. Let's say you land a big client. By facilitating an open conversation and documenting everything that happened—the good and the bad, for the sake of the team—you create a resource for employees who want to capture lessons learned from those who came before them. If you can create the culture, the discipline, and the process for doing so, you will have established an invaluable practice, one that makes the team, and everyone on it, better.

Former marine and retired commander of the Los Angeles Sheriff's Department Sid Heal agrees with John Foley that many leaders don't employ the practice of debriefing in their organizations because they believe it takes up too much time, and he offers his take on its importance: "From their perspective, unless something went drastically wrong, there is nothing more to be gleaned by talking about a situation in the past. Experience may be the best teacher, but it is a harsh schoolmaster, and failing to correct mistakes ensures they will be repeated."[3]

Blue Angels and Navy Seals are disciplined optimizers because the margin for error is small and the ramifications of a single mistake can be catastrophic. The consequences can be disastrous for companies as well. When you optimize, you commit to working with others to reduce or eliminate mistakes. The more people who are involved in the optimizing process, the bigger the reason to have a process to harness skilled discussion. Now, let's look at a process for creating skilled discussions that helps CEOs tackle complex challenges.

ISSUE PROCESSING FOR CEOS

The right atmosphere is rendered more effective when accompanied by a solid process for properly framing whatever issue a CEO may bring to the group. In this forum, CEOs skillfully employ debate, discussion, and dialogue as necessary. The process we'll review, specific to accelerating (versus optimizing), has been used since the late 1950s. By the mid-1970s, it became more widely adopted by peer advisory groups and small business forums throughout the world, and is commonly employed today. While there may be minor variations with the way this model is implemented by other organizations or group leaders, the model itself serves as a meaningful guide for the process you are likely to experience as a member of a CEO peer advisory group. Here's the model, a description of how it works, and examples of the way some smart guides vary its use to inspire the type of skilled discussion necessary for tackling complex issues or opportunities.

GOING WITH THE FLOW

CEOs who bring a particular challenge or opportunity to their peer advisory group for consideration and advice benefit from having a formal process that guides the conversation. These conversations are what Etienne and Beverly Wenger-Trayner call "case clinics." Rather than reviewing a past case study from another company, the group engages in an exercise in which they work on their own challenges in real time. This process is not only helpful for addressing big challenges and answering tough questions, but also, and often more importantly, for pressure testing whether you're actually raising the right question with the group. All too often, the initial question addresses a symptom rather than the real challenge at hand.

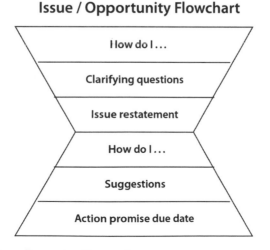

FIGURE 7.1   Issue Processing Protocol

The flowchart, shaped like an hourglass, focuses the individual on the issue at hand by asking "How do I . . . ?" questions. Immediately, just by asking, "How do I?" the individual is encouraged to own the solution. Using the first person—whether you are speaking or writing—promotes ownership, personal involvement, and urgency.[4] Once the question is framed, the CEO explains why the issue is important, what has been done to address the issue to date, and what specific assistance is being asked of group members.

Armed with this information, group members ask *clarifying questions*. This is a very specific form of questioning that helps bring an issue, and the details surrounding it, to light. Over time, CEO members become highly skilled at asking good clarifying questions. For starters, this means that the questions are open ended. If a member asks a closed-ended question (a yes or no question), the member will be instructed to restate it. Another parameter, when forming good clarifying questions, is never to ask a "Why" question. Why questions must also be restated because they tend to elicit defensive responses. For example, don't ask, "Why would you do something like that?" The point isn't to come across as judgmental and put people on their heels; it's to ask questions that will help them open up. Rather than ask a why question, you might say, "Tell us more about that." These simple framing techniques in the clarifying question phase of the process help create a more positive and robust skilled discussion.

Clarifying questions enable the group to understand what the person thinks the problem is, and after hearing all the details the individual describes, the group members can ask themselves, and therefore ask the individual, "What are the symptoms, and where is the root cause of the problem?" If they ask enough questions, they can help a CEO distinguish between an ancillary issue and the core issue.

"After asking questions and listening carefully, it's appropriate for group members to ask, 'Has the individual asked the right question?' People in the room are often very quick to answer, 'Yes, that's the right question,' or, 'No, it's not the right question. Here's what the right question is.' Then, they refocus the individual on the root cause," Jeannette Hobson said. Regardless of how certain a CEO may be about the appropriateness of the initial question, the group helps the CEO dig deeper. They work together so that the CEO and the group can address the real situation at hand.

In a conversation with a former CEO group member, Leo learned how this member discovered he was asking the wrong question and how asking the right one completely changed the member's approach to growing his advertising agency.

The member came to the group essentially asking the question, "How do I go about increasing the rate at which I add new clients?" He then proceeded to talk about how he was charging some of his top people with specific business development responsibilities and making investments in tools for prospecting new leads. He saw new clients as the path to agency growth, and wanted to be more effective and efficient at bringing them in, so he was looking for ideas from group members about how they do it in their businesses.

As it turned out, there was a CEO in the room who had fired her agency a year earlier because of the fallout that occurred when the agency became so focused on winning new clients that the quality of work suffered. The agency not only lost her company as a client, but lost other clients as well. The member explained that, because the agency people were financially incentivized to win new clients, too much of the work was being pushed to junior-level people. She saw a noticeable drop in the quality of the service, as well as the work. Despite repeated warnings, nothing improved, and she had to let them go. The more clients the agency lost, the more difficult it became to add news ones—and because the agency started losing business, many of the top people jumped ship as well.

As group members continued to ask clarifying questions about what the CEO really wanted, they helped him discover he was asking the wrong question. New clients are not the only source of agency growth, and the more the group asked questions and shared their experiences, the more he realized that keeping his current clients, inspiring opportunities for organic growth where possible, and improving the agency's reputation for great creative work and client service excellence could make his firm a magnet for new clients and talented people. Growth would happen not by taking resources from existing clients but by doubling down on them. With the help of the group, the CEO shifted the question from one that focused on winning new clients to one concerned with achieving a more holistic form of sustainable growth.

The member's agency is thriving today because he rededicated his resources to the clients that helped build the agency from the start. By doing so, his clients' businesses grew, they began spending more money, and the quality of the work caught the attention of both clients and fresh industry talent, who were drawn to the agency.

Interestingly enough, this process and the lessons learned in the group not only enable more valuable conversations and interactions, but also give CEOs practices they take back to their own companies and affect the way they lead in their own organization.

Once the group is convinced that the member is asking the right question, the member restates the question—there may then be an additional round of clarifying questions. When the group is satisfied that they have all the information, each member is invited to share her insights or ideas with the member. The member who is bringing the issue to the group sits silently and responds simply by saying, "Thank you." Like the Blue Angels' traditional phrase "Glad to be here," a simple thank-you acknowledges a level of appreciation for a fellow CEO's advice and commitment to the member's success, whether the advice is taken or not. The process continues until every member who wishes to address the issue has done so.

In some cases, a member will volunteer to take notes for the CEO receiving advice so that the information is heard more effectively and captured for further review. After gathering everyone's thoughts, the CEO will be asked to tell the group what he heard and share thoughts about next steps. Those intentions are recorded in writing and revisited at the next meeting so that the member can talk about the actions he took. This process not only creates valuable interaction, but also sets the stage for a culture of accountability, the fifth and punctuating factor, which we will cover in chapter 8.

VARIATIONS ON A THEME

The issue processing protocol provides a framework that is extraordinarily valuable for people to learn, because it teaches them to slow down and think about what they don't know and what they need to know before making a decision. Many different types of issues come up in a CEO group. When the issue is a personal or potentially emotional one, smart guides often employ signature techniques to explain their purpose.

One such technique is called the *fishbowl*. The fishbowl involves starting the conversation with a member and a small number of CEOs inside a circle (the fishbowl) actively working the issue according to the process, while the remaining CEOs sit outside the fishbowl to listen and gather data. After a period of time, the outside group switches with the inside group, so the "outsiders" take what they've heard and observed and inject it into the process. Often, this group offers much better questions, and after this group has a chance to engage the member, the inside and outside groups rotate again. The person in the middle, who has brought the issue to the group, is afforded the opportunity to engage in deep conversations with a smaller set of members in stages rather than working with the whole group at once.

Another approach is known as the *fly on the wall*. After the clarifying questions have been asked and answered, the member backs away from the table, sits silently, and listens. The rest of the members then have a no-holds-barred conversation about the issue and what's really going on. This is where the concept of carefrontation, covered in chapter 5, proves essential. Regardless of the comments, the CEO member understands that this level of honest feedback is rare, and that it comes from a place of caring and from fellow members who want a positive outcome for their fellow CEO. After twenty minutes or so, the person is invited back to the table to join the conversation. This technique offers a powerful way of getting a CEO to look at some aspects of a situation that she has not confronted during earlier meetings.

A third method involves dividing the group into different *perspectives*. Let's say the member wants to acquire another firm. The smart guide will divide the larger group into three small groups. One group may look at the issue from the perspective of the board or the company investors, a second group will examine it from the perspective of the CEO and the management team, and a third group will tackle it from the perspective of family and work–life balance. Each group gathers in different areas of the room and talks, while the member floats around the room to hear the different conversations. The member is not allowed to talk to the groups, only to listen. After enough time has passed, the larger group comes back together and each of the smaller groups shares their perspective. That way, the group covers an issue across three different fronts simultaneously: company, individual, and family.

Regardless of how the issue is processed, from time to time smart guides will ask the people in the room, "Okay, if you were the one who had to solve this problem, what recommendations would you give yourself?" This is where each member expresses what she learned by processing another member's issue. Whether this additional step is taken or not, there is rarely a time when an issue being processed by another CEO doesn't offer valuable takeaways for everyone.

THE FOUR DIMENSIONS

When you combine emotional safety and confidentiality with an intellectual process designed to get to the heart of an issue and elicit honest advice from different perspectives, you create collegiality and a bond that enriches the total experience. Commenting on CEO peer advisory groups from this perspective, Cecelia Wooden of the Hay Group said that this level of skilled discussion takes place in four dimensions: intellectual, emotional, social, and spiritual. According to Cecelia:

> There's certainly the intellectual dimension that is augmented by a group of smart people sharing different experiences and perspectives. The emotional dimension comes from feeling safe to be vulnerable. The camaraderie creates the social dimension, which I believe adds to a person's multidimensionality. Finally, I would suggest that there's a certain spirituality that occurs as a result of fully actualizing your peers, being able to not only emotionally connect with them, but also to have your core values expanded. I regard this as more spiritual than emotional. I'm not talking about religiosity, but spirituality. What is the spirit within me that has grown as a result of those core values, and how can I understand that spirit more? That's even deeper than the emotional bonds that so often occur in such a group.

The degree to which you can learn to look at yourself and your core values through a lens of others, and open yourself to whatever you believe, is amazingly powerful.

SUMMARY

Creating valuable interaction through skilled discussion requires an environment of safety and the firm belief that everything that happens in the room stays in the room. When these interactions happen repeatedly, they create close bonds among group members, who share in the joys of repeated successes. Whether it's the Blue Angels, the Navy Seals, or the members of a high-performing company team, they find excellence in the pursuit of perfection. It's what it means to optimize.

To accelerate with a group of CEOs requires a highly strategic and structured approach. The centerpiece of the process that drives this approach involves a powerful framework that includes properly framing an issue, asking questions informed by experience, and leveraging the power of a collection of successful CEOs. By creating valuable interaction through skilled discussion across four dimensions, the CEO peer advisory group serves as an unparalleled opportunity for personal and professional development. While the first four factors we've described appear to be an effective ensemble, the model gets that much stronger when you add the fifth factor, accountability. It's what makes peer advantage sustainable.

8

Be Accountable

Peter "Pete" Cipollone is cofounder and CEO of InstaViser and was the coxswain for the 2000 and 2004 Olympic U.S. men's eight rowing team. He also won world championships in the men's heavyweight eight in 1997, 1998, and 1999. Pete knows a little bit about winning and the implicit accountability shared by those who are literally *all in the same boat.*

Pete shared a gripping story of personal accountability and what it takes for any team to win Olympic gold. Pete said, "The best example I can come up with is the 2000 Olympics and what came from that experience, brutal as it was. We had been undefeated in the Olympic cycle leading up to the 2000 games in Sydney. We were the heavy favorite to win gold. In the medal race, we came in fifth. Not only did we not win gold, we didn't medal at all. It was just an awful experience for everybody who went through it because for some of those athletes, that was their last go. They would be too old to do it again four years later."

Looking ahead to the 2004 Olympics in Athens, some of the athletes on the team chose not to participate. Some were married with careers and small children, while others simply didn't want to go through another four long years with the possibility of something like that happening again. Pete said, "A few of us chose to continue, and we knew we needed to band together if we were to be the leaders of the next generation." Three members of the Sydney crew qualified to row in the eights at the 2004 Olympics. In the months leading up to the games, there was a lot of peer accountability when it came to team leadership among the three of them. "We accepted the role and rotated it among us. When things weren't going so well for one of us, the others stepped up. Not everybody can be 100 percent effective every day. We didn't talk about it. We just did it. Even now, eleven years later, a lot of the younger guys talk about something that made a big difference for them was that the older guys were always there to be leaders when called upon. If one of our teammates had a concern, they had someone with whom they could talk about it," Pete said.

The veterans of Sydney were on a mission to make sure the mistakes from four years earlier were not repeated. For all of them, whether veterans or first-timers, the goal was to win gold. The personal accountability was palpable but often unspoken. The U.S. men's eight not only won gold in 2004, the team won it decisively.

In this chapter, we'll cover what accountability really means, why it gets a bum rap, what would make CEOs invite more accountability into their lives, and why creating a lasting culture of accountability is arguably the most important factor of all for realizing peer advantage.

WHAT DOES ACCOUNTABILITY REALLY MEAN?

The term *accountability* means different things to different people. What's interesting is that it involves more than just the intellectual denotation and connotation of the word. There's an emotional component that sparks a wide range of reactions when it comes to how a person feels when she is being *held accountable*. For that reason, it may be helpful to spend some time defining accountability and explaining what it means to have a culture of accountability, one that can actually have a positive effect on human behavior rather than an adverse one.

A CEO group smart guide from Colorado, Janet Fogarty explained that when democracy was a nascent form of government in early Greek civilization, citizens cast their votes by stepping on a stone; that's how they would *account* for themselves and demonstrate *where they stand*. Over the years, people have reached their own conclusions about accountability, both in terms of the way they think about it and how it makes them feel. We found that it's not everyone's favorite word. Yet, a number of people we interviewed also believe that accountability has gotten a bum rap, that somewhere along the way, somebody decided that it was a punishment, a form of micromanagement, or mean spirited.

As we explored the various ways people and cultures think of accountability around the world, we discovered a fascinating example from an unusual source. It came from the book *Finnish Lessons: What Can the World Learn from Educational Change in Finland?* Coauthor Pasi Sahlberg has been an ambassador for the country's widely heralded education system. Ranking among the very top in the world in reading, science, and math, Finland's education system emphasizes investment in teacher professional development and spends very little money or time measuring learning outcomes through standardized testing. He stated that, while many countries are demanding accountability, Finland has created a culture in which teachers accept responsibility for teaching their students, and they are given the freedom to do so based on the needs of each individual school and student.[1] In an interview in 2011, Sahlberg noted that there is no word in the Finnish language for accountability, and he described accountability as "something that is left when responsibility has been subtracted."[2] It appears to be such a negative concept in that country that the language avoided a word for it altogether.

Bob Duncan doesn't see accountability as a negative word at all. Commenting on how accountability manifests in CEO peer groups, he said, "I see it as answering a simple question, yes or no, can I count on you? That's how I see it." Members are not there to hold someone's feet to the fire unless they're invited to do so.

One of the CEOs in Bob Duncan's group said to his fellow CEOs around the table, "Do you realize that this is one of the few places where we can go to get support that comes across as unconditional love, unvarnished, with no other strings attached? There are few places where we can go in life where somebody doesn't have an agenda, doesn't want something from us. This is one of the few places where we can show up and hold one another accountable to keep that level of behavior in front of us at all times."

WHAT CEO NEEDS MORE ACCOUNTABILITY?

We've talked to CEOs over the years who say, "I already have enough people to whom I feel accountable professionally. Why would I need to invite more of that into my life?" Former Vistage CEO Rafael Pastor frames the CEO accountability dilemma using the following model.

CEO Accountability Model

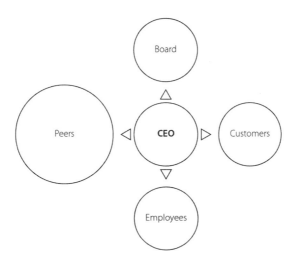

FIGURE 8.1   CEO Accountability Model

Rafael says that a CEO is already being held accountable up, down, and sideways. Looking at the model, you'll see the CEO in the center. The arrow pointing upward looks at people to whom the CEO reports, including the board of directors, shareholders, etc. Rafael calls this ENFORCED accountability. It's enforced in that these groups set certain goals for him: revenues, profits, valuation, growth, international expansion, technological adaptation, etc. They set those goals for CEOs and hold them accountable to achieve those goals.

CEOs are also held accountable by their employees and contractors, people who work for the organization. This EXPECTANT accountability is based on a set of expectations these stakeholders have for their leader. They expect excellent leadership. They expect CEOs to fulfill their promises to them, whether the issue is paying out individual compensation or achieving company goals. They expect the CEO to have a vision for the organization. CEOs are accountable to employees because if the CEO lets them down, they're not going to be happy employees. They will leave or, worse, will stick around grudgingly.

All CEOs also have customers. CEOs are accountable to them because those customers have expectations that the CEO and the company will deliver on their promises. This is called ELUSIVE accountability because the customers are nothing if not discerning. Rafael said, "If I say to you I'm going to deliver a really great toothpaste, I better deliver it. I'm accountable to that to make sure it's good toothpaste at a good price and it's going to taste good to you and going to brighten your teeth. If somebody else comes along with a toothpaste that does all that even better, I may no longer fulfill my promise to you. Customers are fickle, so you better stay sharp."

The three types of accountability described are all imposed on the CEO. So it stands to reason that a CEO might think twice before inviting an entirely new dimension of accountability into the mix. This brings us to the value of the fourth type of accountability. When CEOs are among their peers, they experience EMPATHETIC accountability from people who can relate to being a CEO. What makes this dimension different is not only the dynamic of empathy, but also the fact that it's voluntary. There is no escaping accountability to your shareholders, employees, and customers.

Rafael said, "Peer accountability is entirely voluntary. In my diagram showing 360 degrees of accountability, peer accountability stands out from the others because by being accountable to your peers (peers who understand all the accountability challenges you have with your board, your employees, and your customers), you can deliver better results to those stakeholders. This is the type of accountability that helps CEOs deliver more effectively on the other three. That's the reason top CEOs don't mind volunteering to add yet another dimension of accountability into the mix."

Your CEO peer advisory group acts as a laboratory for personal and professional growth. Rafael noted, "Look, this is a place where you ought to try out as much stuff as you can and it is totally okay to fail; better to fail in here before you show up to the board." One great example of this came from a CEO peer advisory group leader in Malaysia. When Richard Wong started his first group, among his first members was Mag Yoong, chairperson of Cargill Malaysia. She ran the largest organization in his group by far. Cargill had revenues of $1.5 billion at the time, whereas the other group members' companies were in the $50 million to $200 million range, and all of them were run by men. Seeking to expand her business, Yoong wanted to build a container center based at the port, which would require a $55 million investment. She prepared a presentation that she was scheduled give to the worldwide corporate board of directors the day after the group meeting. Richard suggested she deliver her board presentation to the group as a practice run. After first saying no, she finally agreed.

As Richard explains, "The group tore her proposal to pieces, saying that it was too aggressive and too impersonal. With Yoong's permission, they offered their suggestions for resolving the issues. She was clearly taken aback yet grateful for the feedback. When the group took a break, she called her office and told her team to wait until she got back to the office at the end of the day, stating it was going to be a late night and that they had to reinvent their proposal to the board. At the following group meeting, Yoong reported back to the group, telling them that the board members said it was one of the best presentations they had ever seen. When they asked her how she did it, she gladly gave credit to her CEO peer group." The group held her accountable, and she felt a sense of accountability to the group. Yoong trusted the group's judgment, made the necessary changes to her presentation, and happily informed them about the results.

This is just one example of how working with a CEO peer group can help you improve your ability to deliver to the stakeholders who are holding you accountable each and every day. A CEO peer group serves as your accountability practice field.

WHEN ACCOUNTABILITY GETS PERSONAL

Walter Jones and his wife, Debbie, are both architects. After they got married, they started their own architectural firm out of a closet in the bedroom of their first home. Today, they have a $30 million company, and together they have built an organization and raised a family. The couple, their three daughters, and the family dog make an idyllic family portrait. Walter has been a member of a CEO group for eight years, and during that time his members have watched Walter's business grow and his children grow up. Over the years, group conversations touched on personal and family issues as often as they did business topics. During one exchange, Walter revealed that he had done little if anything to set up trusts for his children and get his financial affairs in order, in the event something were to happen to Walter, Debbie, or both. One member asked, "What do you mean you don't have anything? You have the kids. What happens if something happens to you and Debbie? Then what?"

Debbie always wanted to get it done, but Walter dragged his feet. Walter told his members he agreed with their advice and would get right to it. But something always got it the way. Or so he said. And because he didn't regard the matter as urgent, he continued to push it off. Meanwhile, as his group met each month and Walter had not done what he said he was going to do, the group became unrelenting. They continued to raise the issue with him at every single meeting for nearly a year. Toward the end of this period, they even started sending e-mails to Walter saying they would bring tar and feathers to the next meeting if he didn't bring them something to show that he was taking action. Because the members cared about him, they would not let him off the hook. When Walter finally got his financial affairs in order, he shared it with the group and they broke out in jubilant celebration.

A CULTURE OF ACCOUNTABILITY

Many CEOs can relate to Walter and his temptation to put off certain tasks. How many of you have had tasks (or have them now) that you've been meaning to get around to but never quite do? Days become months, and all too quickly months turn into years. Yet, when you finally get around to doing the task you've been avoiding, you realize how simple it is and ask yourself, "Why didn't I do that a long time ago?"

Joseph Ferrari, PhD, a professor of psychology and Vincent DePaul Distinguished Professor at DePaul University in Chicago, is a leading international researcher in the study of procrastination. Ferrari said, "Everyone procrastinates, but not everyone is a procrastinator. We all put tasks off, but my research has found that 20 percent of U.S. men and women are chronic procrastinators. They delay at home, work, school, and in relationships... We are a nation of 'doers' but we are also, like people from other industrialized nations, a people of 'waiters.'"[3]

According to researchers Bruce Tuckman, Dennis Abry, and Dennis Smith, there are fifteen key reasons people tend to put things off:

1. Ignorance: "I didn't know I was supposed to do that."
2. Skill deficiency: "I don't know how to do it."
3. Apathy (1): "I really don't want to do this."
4. Apathy (2): "It really doesn't make any difference if I put this off."
5. Apathy (3): "No one really cares whether I do this or not."
6. Apathy (4): "I need to be in the mood. I'm not."
7. Fixed habits (1): "But I've always done it this way and it's hard to change."
8. Fixed habits (2): "I know I can pull this out at the last minute."
9. Fixed habits (3): "I work better under pressure."
10. Inertia: "I just can't seem to get started."
11. Frail memory: "I just forgot."
12. Physical problems: "I couldn't do it; I was sick."
13. "Appropriate" delays (1): "I'm just waiting for the best time to do it."
14. "Appropriate" delays (2): "I need time to think this through."
15. "Appropriate" delays (3): "This other opportunity will never come again, so I can't pass it up."[4]

In many cases, CEOs will delegate tasks they find uncomfortable, unpleasant, or boring. In other situations, however, when CEOs have to complete certain tasks themselves, they can find the same reasons to procrastinate that everyone else does. When it comes to accountability, CEO peer advisory groups play a particular role in helping CEOs take ownership of tasks and get them done. Time and time again, members say they use their group to publicly declare that they will complete a particular task by a certain date because they know the group will hold them accountable. Even if they do the task just before the meeting date, they've gotten the sense of urgency necessary to spark action. They also know themselves (and their group) well enough to know that, as much as they may loathe an upcoming task, they don't want to have to tell the group they didn't do what they said they would. Though it took Walter a bit longer than the next meeting to get his task done, his group made sure he did it.

There are two aspects of Walter's simple story that are particularly important. One is that the group truly cared about Walter and his family. Their desire to hold Walter accountable for something that he, himself, told the group was important to him was in Walter's best interest. Second, while it's unusual that something like this might take nearly a year, it shows that a culture of accountability involves more than a single follow-up. The group stuck with their member by not giving up on him until the task was completed. Once that happened, they celebrated together not only to acknowledge that Walter had completed the task, but also to show that they were on Walter's side the entire time.

MAKING ACCOUNTABILITY A POSITIVE

Janet Fogarty, said, "As leaders, we're not always good at the skill of holding people accountable. Some of us sound like accusers because no one has ever taught us how to make it a positive experience. Very often, it starts off with an accusation, 'Why haven't you done this?'"

When you use tracking as a stick, it feels like a stick to everyone on the team. Conversely, when you say you are tracking progress in order to help your employees make better decisions, they see the action as giving them the tools to do that. Fogarty added, "It's different for everyone. What gets measured may be what gets done, but I heard somebody else offer that what gets rewarded gets done better. The idea behind tracking is that it ought to be done in a way that people feel a connection to what they are doing and feel as though they are literally playing a role in the company's success."

CEO peer advisory group leader Cheryl McMillan explains that using accountability models can be essential for creating a positive culture of accountability. One of her favorite models is based on the Oz Principle. The Oz Principle defines accountability as "a personal choice to rise above one's circumstances and demonstrate the ownership necessary for achieving desired results: to see it, own it, solve it, and do it." Roger Connors, Tom Smith, and Craig Hickman, in their book *The Oz Principle: Getting Results Through Individual and Organizational Accountability,* developed a vertical diagram with a "line" representing the point of differentiation between victim thinking (below the line or external locus of control) and accountability (above the line or internal locus of control).

Steps to Accountability, or Above the Line Behavior

By following these four steps, you can avoid victimhood.

1. "See It": Recognize and acknowledge the full reality of a situation.
2. "Own It": Accept full responsibility for your contribution to the current experience.
3. "Solve It": Change the current reality by identifying and implementing solutions to your problem while being conscious of Below the Line behaviors if challenges present themselves.
4. "Do It": Fully commit to follow through with the solutions identified, especially when there is great risk in doing so.

The Victim Cycle, or Below the Line Behaviors

1. The Ignore and Deny Stage is where you pretend there is no problem.
2. The It's Not My Job Stage is when you are aware there is a problem and that action is needed. However, you avoid involvement.
3. The Finger Pointing Stage is when you deny responsibility for bad results and shift blame.
4. The Confusion/Tell Me What to Do Stage is when you avoid responsibility by claiming confusion.

5. The Cover Your Tail Stage is when you create stories about why you are not responsible and should not be blamed.

6. The Wait and See Stage is when you know there is a problem that requires action and you choose to not act in the hope that things will magically improve.[5] Leaders who can keep their members above the line can create a culture of accountability in their CEO group and their organization.

Greg Bustin, who leads CEO peer groups in Dallas, Texas, wrote the book *Accountability: The Key to Driving a High-Performance Culture*. In it, he identified the seven pillars upon which you can build a culture of accountability. This model is not only effective in his consulting work with companies, it also helps create and nurture a culture of accountability in the CEO groups he leads. Greg says, "CEO peer groups are an accountability support system for winners." The seven pillars are:

1. Character
2. Unity
3. Learning
4. Tracking
5. Urgency
6. Reputation
7. Evolving[6]

Greg says accountability starts with the character of the individual. Then it's about seeing to it that the bonds created among group members are strong, yet never get in the way of a member's primary responsibility for providing honest and unvarnished feedback. Greg says, "It's great that they can go have a beer together or take vacation together. I just got back from group retreats in three different states, Texas, Colorado, and Florida. Everybody had a wonderful time, but at the end of the day you're there as a peer to provide feedback. I think that when you start with people of high character, when you are all agreed that we're there to help each other get better, when you are clear that the only agenda is the other person's success, then you have a very effective peer group."

Being open to learning and coaching is another aspect of accountability because you have to be prepared to listen in order to be accountable. As for tracking, many CEO group leaders track everything from organizational revenue and profitability to group meeting attendance and willingness to present issues to the group. There's a sense of urgency that's created when you bring an issue to the group and the group gives you air time. Then, you as the CEO are expected to make decisions based on what you've heard and report your progress.

Urgency is less about being fast and more about being focused. It's not about speed; it's about priorities. Reputation is what you earn when you exhibit strong character over time. The seventh pillar is referred to as evolving. Greg says, "I recently read an article about Babe Ruth, because we were coming up on the hundredth anniversary of his last game, and one of the things he said was, 'Yesterday's runs don't win today's games.' That's what the evolving pillar is all about. It's understanding that our principles should not change while recognizing our practices may need to change."

LEGACY

Over time, group members will come and go for a variety of reasons, yet it's important that the group always continues to grow. Norma Rosenberg said, "Even when new members come in, if someone leaves, they're leaving an emotional footprint of asking good questions or caring about the other members. It just accumulates. It keeps on going. You don't start over when you get new members. They're growing together and they do have a legacy, an emotional legacy that's been left by former members and being made by current members and it's changing. It's all about getting to a higher level."

CEO peer group leader Patty Vogan added:

> Another part of accountability and the growth of the group involves managing member departures. In my groups, if a member decides to leave, he or she is asked to give three months' notice. And the reason for that is so everybody has

an opportunity to process somebody leaving. We do hellos, as Americans, really, really well; we do not do goodbyes well at all—especially if somebody's leaving because things aren't going as well in their business or because of a personal issue. Our tendency is to run, hide, put it to the side. I've watched people try to do that over the years, and really had to work hard to encourage people to make sure they finished the process. When they do and everybody has an opportunity to say what they've learned from that person and are able to process how it feels with them not being in that group anymore, the person that wanted to run, always, and this is not sometimes, always says to me, "Oh my gosh, thank you for pushing me to do this day. I really learned something about endings that I never knew was important."

SUMMARY

Ken MacLeod, who is president and CEO of TEC Canada and has led a number of CEO peer advisory groups over the years, said, "In the end, you can't force people to be accountable. They either get it or they don't." When you ask experienced CEO peer advisory group members which of the five factors is most important, they'll usually say accountability. This is primarily because—though surrounding yourself with the right people in a safe and confidential setting, with strong leadership and a well-defined process that drives valuable interaction, is essential—accountability is where peer advantage comes to life. It's where the outcomes and takeaways each CEO realizes from the group experience each week truly manifest for them both personally and professionally. It's why they see being held accountable as a positive, why they volunteer to seek it from their peers, and why it leaves a lasting impression on the group. It's every bit the accountability support system for winners that Greg Bustin so aptly described.

The difference between peer influence and peer advantage is that peer influence is an individual pursuit while peer advantage is a group endeavor powered by greater selectivity, targeted strategies for achieving goals, and structured engagement that inspires lasting results. In parts

1 and 2, we offered the four ways we engage our peers and the five factors necessary for realizing peer advantage. In part 3, we'll explore the extraordinary outcomes that peer advantage affords us. These include how peer advantage can help us grow as individuals and why it's so effective in preparing us for the challenges and opportunities that lie ahead.

PART III

Leading with Peer Advantage

9

The Advantage of Individual Growth

In 1985, Jay Steinfeld was forced out as vice president of finance of Meineke Discount Mufflers after the company was acquired by GKN, a multinational British company. An entrepreneur by nature, Jay joined his wife, Naomi, who had started a mom-and-pop drapery and blinds business called Laura's Draperies. In the late '80s and early '90s, they worked from a storefront and visited people's homes, as they helped their customers select and purchase blinds and draperies. Jay launched a website in 1993 that essentially served as an online brochure for the business. By 1996, he realized people were selling things online, so he launched NoBrainerBlinds.com, one of the early ventures into e-commerce.

In 1997, Naomi was diagnosed with breast cancer, and she was in and out of remission for a number of years. By 2001, Laura's Draperies had three employees, and NoBrainerBlinds.com had two employees—both businesses were making equal amounts of money. Jay was working seven days a week—working with customers six days a week and handling paperwork on Sundays. Then, in 2002, Jay lost his partner in business and in life, as Naomi lost her battle with cancer.

Jay said, "There I was, after being married twenty-six years. I had an extremely happy marriage and three great kids. [All of a sudden] I'm alone with my business, alone with my kids. I'm alone. How am I going to live and be hopeful? It was dismal. It was bleak."

Jay started reading books on philosophy and self-help—anything he could find that might offer him and his children hope for the future. What he learned was to accept that personally—and professionally— life is always a mixed bag of pain and happiness.[1]

In 2004, Jay launched Blinds.com. After a year or so went by, Jay realized that if he were ever to grow and scale the company, he would benefit greatly from the advice and assistance of other CEOs. So in November 2005, he joined a CEO peer advisory group.

Jay's fellow CEOs helped him realize that he couldn't do it all— that being CEO didn't mean he had to be "chief everything officer." He really understood the blinds business, but he had a great deal to learn about being CEO. Over time, Jay's peer group helped him hone his skills in the areas of hiring, coaching, and setting the right expectations for his employees. His personal discipline and hard work created a cultural change that became a foundation for organizational change— and rapid growth—at Blinds.com.

What began with a $1,500 investment nearly twenty years earlier grew to become the world's number-one online window coverings store, with more than $150 million in revenue. The company earned accolades for its company culture, including "Best Place to Work in Houston," "Top 50 Workplaces in Texas," and one of the "Top 50 Most Engaged Workplaces in America." Jay remarried in 2013, and in January of 2014, Blinds.com was acquired by Home Depot.

While Jay ran a profitable business, he idled in owner/operator mode and recognized he needed help to take his business to the next level. Jay took the leap to engage with his peers and change his frame of mind. He learned that rather than spending his time handling specific processes and tasks, he could delegate these responsibilities and focus instead on strategy, the future, and what it means to be a good CEO. Jay's business success and individual growth have gone hand in hand, and ten years later, he remains a dedicated member of his CEO peer advisory group.

In this chapter, we'll talk about how CEO peer advisory groups do more than simply help you grow your business. A good CEO peer group will challenge your worldview, give you pause for reflection, and help you develop as a leader while growing as a person.

CEO GROUPS AS A MECHANISM FOR INDIVIDUAL GROWTH

Individual growth was a hot button for every peer advisory group leader and member we interviewed. Without it, they said, change and the positive outcomes that result from it don't happen. Bob Dabic said, "I've come to the realization that if significant change is going to occur in someone's life, relationships, and business, then the person has to change who they are and who they are being. It's about personal transformation."

People in general hold beliefs about themselves and about how to survive and thrive in life. Most of these beliefs were formed early in life, often in childhood or adolescence. Over time, CEOs who participate in a group begin to identify and recognize those beliefs through their interactions with the other members, and they realize that foundational beliefs that once served them may no longer serve them. It's the beliefs themselves that are self-limiting.

Robert Fritz, known for his development of structural dynamics and his study of the way structural relationships impact behavior, believes that most of us hold two contrary beliefs that limit our ability to create what we really want—powerlessness and unworthiness. Fritz said he's only met a handful of individuals who don't have one or the other, and it's these beliefs that hold you back, regardless of the position you occupy in the organization.[2] That includes the CEO.

Once peer group members become aware of these and other self-limiting beliefs, they can choose to hold on to their beliefs or believe something different. Bob Dabic offered this example:

If someone says, "I must be in control in order to survive," "I must be in control in order to feel worthy," or "I must be in control in order to get great results," something happened along the way that shaped the development of that belief. Once the person realizes the belief is no longer serving her and that it's actually inhibiting her, because she's holding onto too many things, she's not delegating, or she's not working strategically, she realizes that she's got to change. As a result, the person moves from "I must be in control" to "I am trusting of others and worthy of doing that," or whatever their affirmation statement may be. This process sounds easier than it is because while the truth may set you free, it will irritate you first. So it takes time.

Many CEOs find it valuable to identify beliefs that once served them but don't serve them anymore. A peer advisory group can help them face their fears—fear of failure, fear of rejection, fear of emotional discomfort, fear of being wrong—and this is essential for realizing the kind of personal growth that drives real behavioral change. With awareness and choices, members can choose different actions to get better results. It all comes down to whether they want to take a hard look in the mirror and are willing to continue that practice and keep growing. Great group members and leaders will tell you, "Here's what we're noticing, here's what we're seeing, here are some observations to consider, here's some feedback." They don't present it as truth, or as if they are right; instead, they share their perceptions of how you're showing up in a given situation or in other situations.

As any leader knows, you can't separate the business from the personal. They are inextricably intertwined. That's because a human being is running a company, human beings are involved in companies, and people interact with other people. There's no such thing as a purely business issue. Consider an issue such as increasing a line of credit; the CEO may feel fear, anxiety, and risk. Often, emotion permeates business matters.

If you're willing to start with the basic premise that all business issues have some personal aspect to them, and all personal issues have the potential to adversely affect the way you're leading your organization, then you realize the value of bringing your whole self to every group meeting. It's why personal issues come up so frequently in group meetings. CEOs will share their challenges with a child on drugs, a marriage at risk, a family member who's dying, grief over the loss of a loved one, or a health issue. The personal topics up for discussion run the gamut, encompassing all the difficulties leaders struggle with in the course of their lives. If you're going to increase your effectiveness as a leader and enhance your life as a human being, personal topics come with the territory.

Your natural inclination will be that you want to look good in front of your group of CEO peers (not that you need to look good, but you *want* to look good). So when your numbers are off, you don't want to bring your financials. When your numbers are good, you want to bring them. When life is good, you want to share that. When life is not so good, you want to hide it or downplay it. Reflecting on his time as a member, Bob Dabic added that being willing to be vulnerable and bring issues to the group, good and bad, both business and personal, meant that he received real value. "As a member, I received ten to one hundred times ROI for my investment in the group. Today, I tell my members, 'Look, tips and techniques, you get plenty of those, and business-only topics you'll get good input there, but that's a three to ten times ROI, which may be all you're looking for. However, my groups operate at a human being level. If you bring your whole self, you'll receive the ten to one hundred times ROI for your time and dollars invested in the group, just as I once did. That's the path to growth.'"

Many of the stories that follow include the real names of the people and organizations involved, while others have been altered to protect the identity of the individual and the confidentiality afforded to all members, unless they chose to waive it. In either case, we received permission to share these stories in the hope they will help bring the concept of individual growth to life. Here are the members' experiences that made the topic of individual growth very real for them—most of the stories are told by the CEO group leaders in their own words.

RELEASING COMMAND AND CONTROL

In 1997, Ng Chong Lam was general manager of Malayan Electro-Chemical Industry Co., Sdn Bhd (MECI). He was well versed in all aspects of the company's core business in PVC resin and compound products. But he knew he had a shortcoming as a leader. Chong Lam wanted to get the most from his staff, but because of his dogmatic, command-and-control style, the response he received most often from his team was, "Yes, boss." "There was a gap between us," Lam recalled. His subordinates kept their distance and would kowtow to his proposals.

Then he tried emulating the CEOs in his peer group. One idea he borrowed was using incentive trips to reward top-performing staff. He studied the concept for his sales team and devised sales targets that tied in with such trips. He learned that the key to people skills is building relationships. "Trust them and delegate responsibilities, let them make their own decisions," he said. As his group leader Richard Wong explained, it took two to three years for Chong Lam to change his dogmatic style.

As Chong Lam's leadership style improved, so did his personal health. He was less easily agitated and became a calmer person. His cholesterol and stress levels dropped. He even started practicing the principles of Buddhism.

"What you see happening with the personal growth when it comes to leadership style is you'll have a command-and-control guy who sees a CEO peer taking more of a servant leadership approach. When members see the results the CEO is getting, it definitely influences how they approach their teams back at the office. It's a more passive learning experience, but it can be very effective," said Wong.

GAINING CONFIDENCE

When Jane joined a peer group in Texas five years ago, her trucking company was worth $5 million. Today, it's worth $25 million. The consummate learner, she is always improving herself. She also works to improve her processes, her systems, and her structures. Jane constantly asks herself, "What did I do to cause that? What can I do to change that? What can I do better?" She's always seeking outside guidance.

Her smart guide, Robin Stanaland, shared that five years ago Jane lacked confidence, and it showed:

> She was unsure, second guessing, and didn't really want to open up to people around her who were more experienced than she was. She has a reactive personality, because she's an entrepreneur but...now

I would say she is a lot less reactive. She's gained some confidence through her successes. She's still not the most confident in herself, but she doesn't tell everybody about it. She's much better at being an imposter, which I think can be important. I think it's important that she doesn't share so much of her insecurity with her team back at the office. That's what the group is for. That's where you can safely share your insecurities and open yourself to learning.

Because she's now a more confident leader, she's hired people better and smarter than she is, and she's more willing to hold herself accountable. When she has failures it's not the end of the world. She's willing to own it, and instead of saying, "We screwed up!" she says, "I'm the owner of this business. I made this decision. I screwed up." Her personal growth journey, which was fueled largely by learning to trust her fellow members, model their behaviors, and take those behaviors back to the office, played a huge role in driving her business results—without a doubt.

SHARED GRIEF

In another of Robin's groups, a member shared with the group that he had little time to live. As Robin explained:

This was a huge personal growth moment for the group. First of all, it involved dealing with the news of the imminent death of someone close to them. Second, the group had to think about how to manage their own lives, because we had to help shepherd his family, his business, and him through this. Walking with him through the last days of his life really resulted in a lot of personal growth for that group. It forced everyone to get real, look in the mirror, and consider whether their own personal affairs were in order—from a legal standpoint, but also from a personal relationship standpoint. You know, do you have all your relationships where you need to have them if you found out you were dying in five days? Because that definitely happened to us—we lived it, walked through it together and it was very painful and traumatic, but I also saw a lot of people grow through the experience, including myself.

We also had a death of a child. One of our members' sons died from a drug overdose, and while no one in the group had experienced the death of a child, many had dealt with drug addiction in their own families. We got the members through it, and we grew as individuals and as a group as a result of having that issue brought front and center for everyone to process.

GROWING INTO THE JOB

Andrew Lynas was twenty-six years old when he became managing director (MD) of a three-generation family business, Lynas Food Service, located in Coleraine, Northern Ireland. He was already business savvy, with some great experience behind him, but he had never been a managing director before. Andrew was looking for outside experience that would challenge him but also encourage him in his new role.

"Becoming MD at only twenty-six was an incredible opportunity for Andrew," said Edmund Johnston, leader of his peer advisory group. "The family business was strong, and he felt privileged to take on the responsibility." Andrew said he was "looking for some experience, some outside voices who would challenge me, keep me accountable but also encourage me in that position." It was at that point he joined his peer advisory group.

As his company grew, Andrew experienced difficulty with work–life balance issues. He felt isolated because he was working long hours. He was becoming stressed and burned out. He knew that he needed to make a change but didn't know what steps he could take. Andrew drew on the experiences of his fellow managing directors around the room, who understood exactly what he was going through. Johnston said:

One thing about Andrew's peer group is that it's a place for straight talk and there's no place to hide. The group likes to get straight to the point; there is a sense of energy and focus at every meeting. The whole group is engaged and rooting for every member to succeed. Andrew now knows that, as a managing director, personal accountability starts with him, and he puts that into practice every day. Today, he looks inward as never before, always asking himself, "How am I doing? Where do I need to improve?"

With the help of his group, Andrew has grown as a leader and as a person. He was able to make the changes that he needed to bring balance back into his life, which has led him to make better strategic choices. All this has made it easier for Andrew to lead a company that has grown to 370 employees, offering 5,500 products to more than 5,000 customers.

LEARNING TRUST

In 2009, in the midst of the economic downturn, one group helped a CEO determine (because the group reviews key performance indicators every other month) that his thirty-five-year-old company was six weeks away from running out of cash and going out of business. That would have put about eighty employees out of work, and the CEO would have lost most of his net worth. They pulled together a tiger team, brought some members into his company, and helped him to cut more costs than he ever thought possible. Today, the company is thriving and cash flow is massively positive.

"He's living the dream life, but he had to transform," said his group leader, Bob Dabic. "He had to trust people. He had to connect with people. He had to be respectful." When the member initially joined the group, he'd had multiple heart attacks. His business had been marginally profitable, and he was a hands-on micromanager. Bob said:

> He had to delegate. He had to monitor results without meddling in the day-to-day tactical transactional decisions and operations. He had to do a massive personal transformation, which wasn't easy. Fast-forward fifteen years, and he's turned over the day-to-day operations to family members and a president who's been with him for roughly twenty years. Today, he's working two to three

days a week. The company's growing, top line and bottom line, at a faster rate than ever. It took years, but he hung in there. And his company, of the 120 or so plus companies I've worked with during my career of leading CEO groups, is probably in the 95th percentile of the best-run companies. It's just amazing.

Another member worked nearly seventy hours a week and was constantly stressed out. He was missing seeing his kids grow up, and his marriage was facing challenges because he was always working. His controlling style of micromanagement added constant stress to his life.

The member's group showed him how to let go, trust, delegate, set goals, and objectives, create vision-mission-values for his company, hold people accountable, and get rid of some people who were no longer a good fit for his culture. He eventually came into the office closer to twenty-five hours a week, of which he worked about twelve to fifteen hours. He shifted from yelling at his staff to rarely raising his voice.

BEING A GOOD TEAMMATE

UConn assistant coach and former player Shea Ralph explained a personal growth moment she had as freshman at UConn:

I'm probably the most stubborn person on the face of the earth. For me, when I got to UConn, I didn't put practice on the pedestal that it should've been. Practice was practice, but I wanted to play in the games. I wanted to play in front of the crowd. I wanted to put the jersey on. That's why I came here. That was my attitude.

When we practice, one of the big things that we emphasize is communication. We constantly ask our players to talk during practice. Talk, clap, encourage your teammates, that kind of thing. I was like, "I'm not doing that. I'll clap every now and then, but that's wasting a lot of energy. I'm about to be out here for three hours, I'm not doing all that." I did not practice well early on, and I specifically remember an incident that happened because of that.

We had an All American named Nykesha Sales, great player, really, really good player... So, we're practicing one day, and she makes a great play, and Coach Auriemma blows the whistle, and he looks at me and he said, "Shea, was that a great play?" I said, "Yeah." He said, "Did you say anything to her?" I said, "No." He said, "Okay."

Three possessions later, she did the same thing, made another great play. He blew the whistle again and said, "Shea, did Nykesha make a good play right there?" I said, "Yeah." He goes, "You say anything?" I say, "No." Next thing you know, Coach says, "All right, everybody, put the balls up on the rack. Clearly, our team doesn't understand what I'm trying to get accomplished here." And he made us all run for forty-five minutes. I was scared to go into the locker room after that. I honestly thought Nykesha Sales was going to end my life that day. From that moment forward, and I'm not kidding you, even now as a coach, I am the most obnoxiously loud person on the court. When it comes to rooting for others during a game or in practice, you will not find anyone louder than me.

BUILDING COURAGE

Barbara had been a member of a CEO group for about twelve to eighteen months. Though she was relatively new, she'd reached the conclusion that she wasn't good enough. Barbara didn't regard herself as an equal in the group. She was a little bit younger, and one of only three women in a group of fourteen. Compounding that, she had a dysfunctional relationship with her business partner that she talked about with the group during some meetings, but she always appeared to be holding something back. Barbara was ready to quit. Her group leader convinced her to bring the issue with her partner to the group one more time, and she reluctantly agreed.

Barbara presented the issue and the fact that she was considering leaving the group. The members responded by letting her know how much progress they believed she had made since joining the group—that she had come a lot further along than she thought. The group also helped her process the partnership issue at a much deeper level, so she could take new ground and get on equal footing with her partner. Barbara was actually running the business, while the partner played largely a passive role and wasn't really much help. After role-playing a meeting with her partner with a group member, she gained the courage and confidence to do what she needed to do. It's a situation Barbara never would have been able to confront eighteen months earlier. Barbara realized she had grown as well.

SUCCESSION GROWTH

When Héctor Polakoff joined his peer advisory group in Buenos Aires in 2006, his big challenge was succession planning for his family business. He wanted to know how to best handle his eventual retirement and pass on leadership to the next generation. Héctor was about twenty years older than most of the other group members, so it took him a few meetings to really open up and share what he was going through. Eventually, the group helped Héctor reveal that one of his primary concerns about walking away from the business was that he feared delegating leadership to his nephew. Just as Héctor was hitting his stride with the group, the group hosted a speaker who led a workshop on succession planning. Héctor was so impressed with what he heard that he hired the speaker, who, with the help of his group, actually accelerated the transition.

During this time, Héctor realized he had to start changing his life habits to better prepare for transitioning out of the company and finding a new role in his life. At a group anniversary party, one of his members challenged the attendees to initiate social change. Héctor accepted the challenge and, with the help of his group, started an NGO. This NGO, Empujar, is now five years old and helps approximately one hundred kids from low-income environments who are finishing high school acquire the skills necessary to get their first job. Today, there are about seventy companies participating in this foundation. Héctor is the president of Empujar and, while he continues as president of his family business, he no longer runs it. Héctor's nephew is now the CEO (and a CEO peer advisory group member himself).

MEETING CHALLENGES AND SEEING THE POSSIBILITIES

Most CEOs join peer advisory groups to help them run healthier companies and grow their businesses. Being part of a group of CEOs from noncompeting businesses allows them to step outside their company and industry to learn how challenges they share are handled by different leaders from different sectors. They understand that taking their company to the next level, whatever level that may be, often requires a different approach than what's been working thus far. As Marshall Goldsmith proclaimed, "What got you here, won't get you there."[3]

Of course, there are various ways to expand your worldview, and iHeartMedia chairman and CEO Bob Pittman realizes that, as a CEO running a company every day, he naturally has blinders on; according to Pittman, the older you get, the narrower your world can become if you don't get out once in a while. Pittman expanded on this idea:

> I go to Burning Man every year. The reason I go to Burning Man is because it's the most radical departure from the life I lead in business that I could imagine. It's great for me because, for a week, I'm seeing the world completely differently. I also like to travel to exotic places and countries. I like to go to Bhutan, where they have "Gross National Happiness" instead of gross national product, and spend a week there just to sense, "Okay, how can I change my perspective?"... I'm interested in the ideas and pushing my own mental boundaries. I think the world would be a lot better place if everybody did that.

Bob takes a different approach to achieving individual growth, but his goal is the same. As successful as Bob has been in his career, he is constantly learning and trying new things—that's likely among the reasons he has realized such success.

Growing your company challenges the bounds of your current thinking. There is no such thing as business *or* personal, because it's business *and* personal. If you're open to learning from your colleagues, the first thing you discover is that growing your organization starts with growing you. Organizational growth will not happen without personal growth. Peer advantage isn't fully realized without it either.

SUMMARY

Confidence, courage, and character tend to reveal themselves during the times that challenge us most. As leaders, these stories offer a fitting reminder that if you expect your people and your organization to grow, the growth process has to begin with you.

In our next chapter, we'll explore how stepping outside your company and your industry can help you see tough challenges and identify opportunities before they're right on top of you. Think of how tough it would be to prepare for a hurricane if all you were able to do was look out the window. Yet when you open yourself to a broader view of the landscape, you can see it coming well in advance and take the steps necessary to brace for its impact. That's exactly what happened during the 2008 financial crisis. The difference between many of the companies that weathered the financial storm and those that did not wasn't that they were necessarily better run companies, they were just better prepared companies. We'll talk specifically about how CEOs worked together to survive the 2008 financial crisis and how your CEO peer group can provide you with the kind of advance notice that will help you meet tough challenges and identify opportunities for your business before it's too late.

10

The 20/20 Vision Advantage

Former MIT Engineering School dean Gordon Brown used to say, "To be a teacher is to be a prophet. We are not preparing children for the world we have lived in but for a future we can barely imagine."[1] The same could be said for CEOs leading and preparing their organizations for uncertain business conditions.

When it comes to broadening your view and expanding your peripheral vision, your peers can bring this to you in a manner that is difficult to access elsewhere. Because we are all players in a complex system, the actions of one person, one company, or one industry tend to create ripple effects across the entire system. When you call upon peers from outside your industry sector to help you better understand the specifics of what's happening in their worlds, you can more easily evaluate the system as a whole, and then assess what that means for you. Your peers will help you meet challenges, seize opportunities, and chart your own course for the future. This is how peer advantage provides you with a vision advantage, which not only allows you to prepare for the future but, more importantly, to shape it.

RECESSION PROOF

The financial crisis of 2008 had a significant impact on most businesses. Nadia Lee, CEO of Adia Kibur, is a sought-after trend consultant and designer, with jewelry in more than two thousand stores nationwide.

Luxuries and accessories were hit especially hard during the recession, and Nadia felt the impact. Fortunately, she reacted quickly by focusing on her designs and making sure they maintained their fashion-forward appeal. Her group encouraged her to travel and maintain a presence at trade shows despite the rising costs and near-term losses to the business. This steady persistence resulted in her securing Macy's as a new client in Q3 2011, as other large retailers took notice of this boutique fashion designer. By collaborating and building relationships with key vendors, Nadia increased her top line by 40 percent in 2012. Her private label line had the highest-selling item both in stores and online. Today, Nadia dictates much of the fashion jewelry designs we see on the market.

In essence, the group functioned as a ready and waiting council able to help her steer her ship through the financial storm. Nadia leveraged the benefits of the five factors of peer advantage to share her struggles, process her issues, benefit from the input of trusted and diverse peers, and be held accountable for moving forward. Nadia, and all CEOs, for that matter, are responsible for knowing what's coming and doing everything possible to meet challenges and seize opportunities.

The more you are able to focus on the future, the greater chance you have of seeing around the corner and finding ways to succeed—whether the economy is in the midst of prosperity or decline. A group helps the CEO take a "view from the balcony" and get early warning signs that can be gleaned by talking to other CEOs from different industry sectors. Without that view, it's all too easy to get caught up in the day to day. This is how leaders get blindsided.

GETTING AHEAD OF A CRISIS

While most people came to understand the root causes of the 2008 recession after the fact, some saw it coming. They didn't know precisely when it would happen or how deeply or broadly it would cut but they did know a storm was looming, and they prepared and responded with the advantage of foresight gained from their peers.

In 2006, a number of CEOs in Atlanta, Georgia, were members of a peer group led by Linda Gabbard. As part of their learning process for looking forward, the CEOs in this group followed the work of an economist with a solid reputation for tracking the ups and downs of the global economy. With signs that a banking crisis was on the horizon, a banker in Linda's CEO group agreed that it was just a matter of time before the music stopped playing and everyone would be scrambling for a seat. A correction was in the air—and would likely come in late 2008 or 2009. Other members, whom Linda describes as leaders of companies in bleeding-edge industries, were also feeling some shakiness in their markets. The economic forecast, along with evidence brought to the group by members representing a broad range of industry sectors, prompted them to take action. As a result, they made two important decisions: (1) do everything possible to prepare, and (2) stick together and help one another weather the storm, no matter what.

In order to prepare, the group agreed to dedicate more time to working on this issue together. For eight of their twelve monthly meetings, they typically invited guest speakers to conduct half-day presentations or workshops on topics relevant to the priorities of the group. They decided to reduce the number of speakers from eight to six so they could spend more time working together in what they called their executive sessions. For the six speakers, they invited experts they believed could be most helpful in their preparations for the upcoming crisis.

The banker in the group led his fellow CEOs through a series of exercises. For example, any CEO who relied on a credit line was asked to create a presentation for her banker. Everybody had a plan A, plan B, and plan C. Plan A was based on the scenario, "I'm going to stay with my current bank." Plan B was based on the idea, "I've got to change banks." And because it was possible that the company's current bank could go under, plan C essentially prepared for this scenario: "What would happen if I couldn't get a line of credit?"

Every CEO who was credit-line dependent, which was most of them, developed a presentation for each of the three scenarios. As a result of proactive management of their banking relationships, every company was able to either keep its financing or get new financing. "Most of them had multiple offers they could choose from. This was in a time when nobody could get credit," Linda said.

The group also realized that, as hard as it would be to continue to invest time and money in their CEO group during a financial crisis, they needed one another most during these difficult times. In order to "stick together and weather the storm, no matter what," they agreed that this was no time to leave the group or take a break from it. When the worst of the recession had passed, every CEO's company had survived, and all are thriving today.

RAISE YOUR HEAD OUT OF THE BOAT

Nathan Bennett and G. James Lemoine wrote an article for the January–February 2014 issue of *Harvard Business Review* titled: "What VUCA Really Means for You." VUCA is an acronym that emerged from the military in the 1990s and has since become popular when discussing strategy for all types of organizations. It's a catchall reminder that as we look to the future, we do so in a world filled with volatility, uncertainty, complexity, and ambiguity. Bennett and Lemoine warn against using this characterization of the world as a crutch or an excuse for not looking to the future and planning accordingly. As they note in the article, "After all, you can't prepare for a VUCA world right? Actually, you can."[2]

German military strategist Helmuth von Moltke once said, "No battle plan survives contact with the enemy."[3] In business, you might say no business plan survives contact with the customer. There are always unknowns. Dwight Eisenhower noted, "In preparing for battle, I have always found that plans are useless, but planning is indispensable."[4] No matter how uncertain the future or how unpredictable you may regard certain events, Bennett and Lemoine suggest that it shouldn't "throw off the hard work of strategy and planning."[5]

If you talk to people who race sailboats, they'll tell you that no two races are ever the same—there is different wind, weather, equipment, competitors, etc. Sailboat racers say that to win, you have to get your head out of the boat.[6] This essentially means that while it helps to look at the instruments that measure speed, wind, and direction, it only matters relative to the other boats in the race. Working with a diverse group of CEOs is a way to get your head out of the boat, to stop working in your business and start working *on* your business. It means facing all the volatility, uncertainty, complexity, and ambiguity that the world can throw your way with a plan for the future that considers a wide range of scenarios and focuses squarely on agility—the antidote to the VUCA world.

Mike Richardson, who has been guiding and speaking to groups for more than ten years, told us that he challenges his CEOs to face the future head on: "I ask them: How are you going to future proof yourself? How are you going to be recession ready? How are you going to do all of that in an increasingly time-compressed world that is accelerating all the time? If you think it's difficult now, just wait twelve months or even twelve weeks."

Richardson believes strongly that the only advantage that has any permanence these days is agility. "Everything else is increasingly temporary," he says. "If you want to have an agility advantage, you better damn well have a peer advantage because they are inseparable. The best place to develop that advantage of agility is in a group of your peers, which is filled with such diversity and such a good process that it actually gives you a fighting chance to survive and thrive in the VUCA world."

WHAT SHOULD YOU BE PAYING ATTENTION TO?

Richard Curtin is a research professor and the director of the Thomson Reuters/University of Michigan Surveys of Consumers at the Survey Research Center, Institute for Social Research. He also codirects the University of Michigan's national Panel Study of Entrepreneurial Dynamics. Curtin says that the key to ascertaining what will take place in the future is understanding what's happening with consumers: "CEOs need to broaden their view when they think of the economy. Most think in terms of macro trends, income, sales, and profit ratios, or something like that. I think that the better way of thinking about it is to consider it all from the customer's perspective. How do they see their own situation? How are they making their decisions?" Curtin adds that the more a CEO becomes exposed to customers in industries outside

her own, the more objective she can be and the more likely she is to spot
trends that can guide future decision making.

Curtin said, "You have a distance from their situation, and that
distance allows you to become more objective, and discover underlying trends that wouldn't have been obvious to you if you just talked
to someone who knew your lingo, understood your background, and
talked about business conditions in the same way you do. Working with
your peers outside your industry is an extremely effective way of gaining
that perspective."

Looking at macro data is like trying to drive your car forward by
looking through the rearview mirror. What happened in the past, or
even dominated in the past, doesn't offer much guidance about what's
going to happen tomorrow. The CEOs, economists, and group leaders
with whom we spoke said that for guidance about the future, you have
to look at different sources of data, at how people are living their lives,
what they're demanding, and what kinds of products and services they
are gravitating toward. Young people today have become less focused
on products and much more attentive to service, which extends to both
housing and vehicles. Curtin said, "Twenty to thirty years ago, houses
and cars were the primary goods that most every consumer desired."
Young people today often want the flexibility and mobility that come
with renting versus owning, or they are happy to utilize services like
Uber or Zipcar to meet their transportation needs rather than buying
a car. Meeting the challenges of the future will involve understanding
what your next generation of customers wants. That means you have to
think more like a futurist.

THINKING LIKE A FUTURIST

Sheryl Connelly, corporate futurist for Ford Motor Company, agrees
CEOs need to pay attention to the needs and desires of their customer:
"Blue jeans have been around for roughly 150 years. In the early 1900s,
if I tried to walk into a fine hotel wearing blue jeans, I wouldn't get past
the front door. Jeans were worn by laborers. They were low cost and
highly utilitarian. Today, they are high fashion. They are common in

many office environments, and I could wear them at just about any fine restaurant. What changed in the last 100 years were our values, attitudes, and behaviors. This is what CEOs need to pay attention to."

Connelly suggests that the SWOT analysis remains an important strategic planning tool in most organizations today. The SWOT, of course, is a framework for assessing an organization's strengths and weaknesses and identifying the opportunities and threats present in the marketplace. The problem with the SWOT analysis is that it's extremely limiting. For example, you can ask yourself what you do well and list your strengths, but Connelly would argue that you do not own your strengths, your customers do. They are the ones who decide what you're good at, and they can be extremely fickle. Another way it's limiting is that CEOs can get blindsided by the unlikely competitor—the one they never would have considered. Blockbuster and Kodak are perfect examples. Blockbuster's retail model was obliterated not by another brick-and-mortar retailer, but by technology and the advent of streaming video. Kodak was a casualty of the digital age as well. During the early '90s, commercials that defined life as a series of "Kodak moments" sold the importance of capturing and saving those precious snapshots of our lives on film. Altimeter Group principal and best-selling author Brian Solis redefines the "Kodak moment" for a new generation as that moment in time when a company fails to respond to changes in technology trends, the needs of the marketplace, or the desires of its customers, only to be left behind. Kodak fell victim to its own unwillingness to take digital technology (which it owned, by the way) to market because it mistakenly thought Kodak was in the film business and didn't want to cannibalize sales. The "Kodak moment" went from a precious snapshot of life to a cautionary tale. How's that for a change in consumer values, attitude, and behavior?

Rather than use a SWOT to look inward, broaden your view and focus on what you can't control that could affect your business. Use a mechanism for staying abreast of social trends, technological advances, economic drivers, environmental concerns, and political dynamics. Consider what Sheryl Connelly describes as "wild card events," such as 9/11 or the 2013 earthquake in Japan. While neither could have been predicted, 9/11 instantly raised deep concerns over the United States's dependence on foreign oil, which affected values, behaviors, and attitudes associated with buying gas-guzzling SUVs. In the case of Japan's 2013 earthquake, Japanese government and business leaders had contingency plans in place to ensure the survival of their organizations, because they are geographically vulnerable to earthquakes. Those companies doing business in Japan, however, were less prepared for the disruption. For a number of those companies, it took years to recover.

One popular approach to planning for circumstances and situations beyond your control is scenario planning: instead of looking inside, you begin with the 100,000-foot view. It's when you ask yourself all the "What if?" questions about circumstances beyond your control. You create what Connelly calls bookends—best- and worst-case future scenarios, along with two others that fall in between. If your plan puts you in position where you can pivot and be prepared for whatever actually happens, then you probably have a pretty good plan.

Scenario planning, created by futurist Herman Kahn in the 1950s, has proven quite effective,[7] as researchers from Bain have shown steady high satisfaction levels in surveys conducted over a twenty-year period since 1993.[8] The value of scenario planning is that it takes you outside the framework of your organization and forces you to challenge your most basic assumptions. The problem with underlying assumptions is that they are so buried beneath the surface of our consciousness and so nonnegotiable, you can barely identify them let alone challenge them. Scenario planning and thinking like a futurist tends to be quite powerful for CEOs because, with the diversity of perspectives and challenges shared by the group members, they have the ability to ask the kinds of good questions that get to the heart of those assumptions. This allows you to look at assumptions and see if they are still holding up in the changing landscape. The group members rely on one another to identify what they are missing and find opportunities embedded in challenges.

PROCESSING OPPORTUNITIES

Mike, CEO of a Denver-based commercial electrical contracting company, had revenues of nearly $15 million prior to the 2008 financial crisis. As Mike was in the process of hunkering down, his peer advisory group—which included a member who manufactured solar panels—talked to him about using this time to explore adding solar installation to his menu of commercial services. Seven years later, Mike's company has revenues of more than $100 million, and he's the third-largest solar installer in the United States. Mike agreed to explore what was possible, and his group gave him the courage and the benefit of their insight to try it.

When you engage in rich conversations with a group of people you trust, exploring opportunities you would otherwise have never imagined seems less daunting. The group serves as a mechanism for driving conversations that give everyone a sense that anything is possible—once that happens, the plausibility of success seems higher. These conversations with fellow CEOs inspire questions such as: What's the probability of these particular pieces? What things have to happen to raise the probability? What things could get in the way? The longer the idea survives CEO scrutiny, the more likely the member is to step up and say, "I'm going to try this."

Mike's company, for example, started installing solar panels on a small scale and eventually moved to bigger installations. As his group leader, Chris Noonan, put it, "Drive down in the Palm Springs area and south, and you'll see his handiwork. It's a success story not just for Mike but for the entire group, because Mike's results have inspired other CEO group members to look outside their core strengths for future opportunities—opportunities they would have never considered just a few years earlier."

Fred Chancy leads a group called TEC 7, so named because it was the seventh CEO peer group launched by TEC back in the 1960s. Although many of its members are retired now, the group still meets regularly. Fred says that whether times are good or challenging, you have to be sure you're having the right conversations and paying attention to what really matters—focusing on opportunities. With every problem, there's an opportunity waiting for you. Some are more obvious than others, so it helps to have peers who will help you look.

Fred traces this approach back to Peter Drucker, who wrote about the very simple idea that it's more important to be working on the right thing than to "be trying to do everything right." The single most important decision that we make as individuals, and certainly as CEOs, is choosing what we're going to work on or think about. The president of the United States and the heads of the largest corporations in the world all have the same number of hours in the day. Different people choose to think about and work on different things, and that's really what makes the difference between great leaders and average ones.

Fred was also struck by an article he read years later on why MBAs seldom become effective CEOs. According to the piece, the reason is that they tend to be problem focused. Because they learned how to use these analytical tools in business school, they tend to seek problems and then put their analytical tools to work. Quoting Peter Drucker, Fred said, "If you solve all the problems in a company, where does that get you?" Fred notes:

> A very successful CEO once told me, "The biggest mistake that most CEOs make is they put their best people on their biggest problem instead of putting them on their biggest opportunity." As I see it, if you identify one single opportunity, it often can transform a company and change everything for the better. I think an excellent example of that would be Steve Jobs. When he came back to Apple, they had more problems with their computers, and he could have spent the rest of his life working those problems. Instead, he chose to focus on opportunities and products like the iPod, and he changed the way we listen to music. The iPad and the iPhone changed the way the whole world communicates.

Another example of looking at opportunities involved a defense contractor that had 95 percent of its work coming from the federal government. The company had created and developed technology that was significant for the government, particularly at a time when the U.S. was involved in multiple international conflicts.

Later, with government sequestration and a sluggish economy, the company found itself with technology in search of a customer. With the help of his peer group, the CEO explored what was possible in a world that bore no resemblance to the one in which the company had been thriving just a few years earlier. Together, they explored fields and industries outside the government, and outside the warfare arena (a pretty niche area), that might make some use of the technology the company had developed.

Today, the company not only works with air traffic control, it has also expanded into the medical devices industry. Surgeons use the company's technology to help them operate with greater precision and to see areas of the human body that they had not been able to see into before. The entire shift in the company's customer base inspired the development of new and exciting products that would never have been created had the CEO not had the benefit of peers who could help him see the broader landscape.

Looking at another example, the managing partner of a boutique law firm in Atlanta was a peer group member. When he joined the group, he was very keen on learning and broadening his perspective, but he was not interested in adding to the firm's ten attorneys. His attitude was, "This is it. I don't want to be bigger than this. This is what my firm is. I just want to learn more and do better with what I've got but we're never going to be any bigger." Then one of the group members, a franchisor, walked up to the attorney during one of the meeting breaks and said to him, "Your business model would be really easy to make work well as a franchise." That one comment triggered a change in the member's mindset. He later brought the idea to the group, and they helped him assess the opportunity and create scenarios for what could be possible if he ultimately chose to go in that direction. Today, the firm has more than twenty attorneys, and it's engaged in four brand new lines of business.

BRINGING PEERS TOGETHER FOR GLOBAL IMPACT

Hazel Henderson, a futurist who has been bringing smart people together for decades, said that with all of the new technologies we have created, we actually need to connect the dots. She sees the challenge as "the reintegration of knowledge," because there's really no way of going forward on one small planet without truly understanding the ways all these different sectors interface with one another and how technologies amplify or suppress one another. Henderson said:

> It's the kind of stuff I did when I was a science policy wonk in Washington for six years at the U.S. Office of Technology Assessment. We were doing pretty much nothing else except creating broader matrices where you could actually look at all of the consequences of these individual strategies of individual sectors and individual companies, and ascertain their social and environmental impacts. That was actually the charge of the office, and we produced a tremendous number of very anticipatory studies which were quite upsetting to the existing sectors of the economy, which we now refer to around here as "legacy sectors." They're the fossil fuel sectors, and that would include the automobile sector and the chemical agriculture sector.

Hazel Henderson, who has authored nine books and whose editorials appear in twenty-seven languages and in two hundred newspapers around the world, founded Ethical Markets Media in 2004. "We convene groups of people," Hazel said. "What we are doing today is bringing together pioneer asset managers. At our last conference for example, we brought together asset managers for pension funds mostly, people who had created successful, profitable, fossil fuel–free portfolios. They needed to talk to each other, because every one of them thought that they were totally alone and that there was nobody else out there. Of course, their colleagues were blaming them for all kinds of things, you know, the drop in oil prices and everything else, and they were saying, 'No, no, no. You have to have a broader model to understand what's happening.' This is exactly what we do."

Mike Klowden is the CEO of the Milken Institute. The Milken Institute is a nonprofit, nonpartisan think tank determined to increase global prosperity by advancing collaborative solutions that widen access to capital, create jobs, and improve health. A good deal of the institute's charge involves the policy work in Washington and research in the fields of health and finance, but it is best known for bringing people together to look at the world in a different way.

Mike said:

> We're bringing people together who otherwise might not talk to each other or might not hear certain types of ideas because they just stay in their own silos. We try to get them to break out of their silos to work together and get things done. We do it in a totally nonpartisan way, which is relatively unique for think tanks.
>
> The contacts we secured through our global conference enabled us to attract people to come to our smaller convenings. These people may meet at the larger gathering and come up with an idea worth pursuing. They use the smaller convenings to continue what they started at one of our larger conferences. As the global conference started to grow, we expanded the number of sessions and panels. We started out mostly with economics and finance, and we expanded it to include more health, more philanthropy, a little more into politics, and technology and education.

The conference has grown from twenty-eight sessions to more than two hundred sessions with seven hundred speakers the past year on a variety of topics. While the largest group of people who come are still interested in finance or interested in the area that they work in, they attend a variety of sessions. "One of the things I'm most pleased about," Mike said, "is that people tell us that by going to other sessions, they heard ideas that they never would have had, that they were able to use in their business or to profit their foundation, whatever, and that's always very exciting to us."

SUMMARY

When you were a child, you might have sat (or even stood) on the shoulders of an adult and enjoyed the view that came with your newfound increase in height. For that brief time, you could see and appreciate more about your surroundings. In a CEO group, you stand on the shoulders of your fellow members—CEOs who lift you up to catch a glimpse of the world for a better view. It's a view you see not only from your own perspective but through their eyes as well. The trust and mutual respect you share give you permission to challenge one anothers' assumptions, see opportunities where others see problems, exchange ideas that, while commonplace in one industry, may be unheard of in another, and embrace new ways to work toward a brighter future.

A peer group meeting is the place where you can think like a futurist—balancing provocation with plausibility—to plan for the best and the worst and to have the agility necessary to handle whatever the VUCA world has to offer. It's where you will not only contemplate the future but also work to shape it by preparing your organization to thrive in that world we can barely imagine. As the CEO, this is your responsibility. It's what Fred Chaney described as working on the right things. Now you just have to find the right peers with whom you can share your aspirations.

11

The Power of Peer Advantage

In 1961, Don Guild owned a small drugstore in southern California with his dad; soon, they opened a second, larger store. From that point on, Don opened a new store every year or so until he eventually reached thirteen stores. In 1969, he joined Fred Chaney's TEC group to work with other CEOs and small business owners who were trying to build their businesses. Over the years, Don faced a constant struggle: he was trained as a pharmacist but he hated being a pharmacist. By 1982, when CVS started opening stores in Southern California, Don began to wonder if this could be his shot at getting out of the pharmacy business once and for all. A year later, CVS contacted Don about buying his thirteen drugstores. Soon after, Thrifty Drug called him because it also wanted to expand into the region. Now he had two companies vying to buy his small chain. Both companies were seeking to open many stores in a short period of time and use their newly acquired sales and customer base to advertise aggressively and achieve market dominance. Don consulted his group about how to go about selling his stores.

In 1984, Don prepared an operating statement and a balance sheet and brought them to his monthly TEC group meeting to review with his fellow members. Based on the numbers, Don planned to sell Guild Drug for just under $10 million. One of his fellow members, Red Scott, was running a public company called Intermark at the time. Red, along with a few other members, reminded Don that both drug store chains were interested in buying Guild Drug for strategic reasons. While his company had a good bottom line, neither chain was buying his stores for that reason alone. It was about market position and a race to capture the dominant position first. Don's fellow group members told him, "We think you ought to double the price you're going to ask." As Don told us:

> A couple weeks later, I met Thrifty Drug CEO Leonard Straus and his chief operating officer for lunch on Wilshire Boulevard. After a few moments of small talk, Leonard asked me, "What do you want for the chain?" I gave him the figure my members recommended, and he just reached over with his hand and said, "Okay. We got a deal." Oh my gosh, I thought! It was double what I told the group I would have sold it for during our meeting just a few weeks earlier. If it hadn't been for the counsel I received from my group members, I would have given up millions.

Don not only joined a peer group and sought their advice, he had such a deep trust and respect for his members that he accepted the advice and took it with him to his lunch meeting. Don put his financial life in their hands, and he was a big winner as a result.

Don experienced the power of peer advantage. He carefully selected the group and came to realize that it was a safe and confidential environment for sharing his most sensitive issues (both personal and professional). He trusted the group's leader, Fred Chaney, and all of his fellow members. They had a disciplined approach to dialogue that effectively pressure tested any and all recommendations and often uncovered new ways of interpreting the same situation. The group's perspective was worth roughly $10 million to Don, and his group members all shared in Don's joy. That's how accountability looked on that day—not as a negative, just a big plus. Forty-seven years later, Don is still a member of his group. His primary residence these days is Hawaii where, well into his eighties, Don remains an avid surfer. He flies to Southern California every month to attend his group meeting and has no plans to quit anytime soon.

WHAT ACCOUNTS FOR THE MAGIC OF PEER ADVANTAGE?

As we've discussed, peer advantage is not an individual activity, it's a group endeavor. It's what's possible when you bring great people together who want to chase perfection in the pursuit of excellence. Groups like the Blue Angels, the Navy Seals, and UConn's women's basketball team understand what it means to optimize. For them, there is no such thing as the perfect flight, the flawless mission, or the error-free game.

CEO peer advisory groups are shining examples of what's possible when people are committed to accelerating their growth—to stepping outside their company and industry to see beyond the limits of their individual perspective so they can learn, grow, and meet the challenges of an uncertain future. These groups involve high-performing CEOs dedicated to developing themselves and their organizations, and they are committed to helping their fellow members succeed. The Japanese proverb "None of us is as smart as all of us" is a fitting reminder that, while you could choose to go it alone, there's no need to. And if you don't have to, why would you?

Each of the five factors necessary for experiencing peer advantage stands on its own. No one factor is more important than another. But if you're looking for the magic, you won't find it in any single factor—or in any combination of a few, for that matter. Think of each factor as one instrument of a five-piece jazz ensemble. Remove one instrument and the magic is gone. Only when all the instruments are playing their parts does the ensemble create that magical sound.

Interestingly enough, there are two other ingredients to the magic that we discovered during our study from the peers we consulted to write this book. Beyond the ensemble of five factors, there's the power of the triad. In chapter 6, we leveraged Dave Logan's research to describe the group not in terms of a hub and spoke or as a group leader in front of an audience of CEOs, but as a triad. This is where a relationship of trust and caring is held equally by the leader, the individual member, and the group itself. Each has responsibility for "having the relationship's back," so to speak. It's an invisible overlay that gives the five factors their strength.

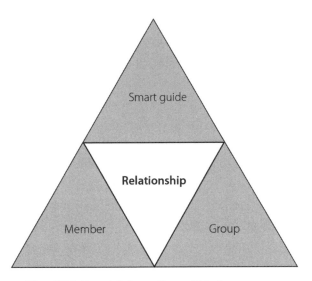

FIGURE 11.1   The CEO Peer Advisory Group Triad

Finally, the magic comes from the people. It's where experience and spontaneity create extraordinary moments of kindness, wisdom, creative genius, and understanding, to name just a few. When we talked to UConn assistant coach Shea Ralph, she acknowledged that excellent coaching and a great culture can set the stage for success, but at the end of the day, it comes down to individuals who need to make plays. Time and time again, in the stories we've shared from groups around the world, the five factors and the strength of the triad created the conditions for success; at the end of the day though, success came down to someone in the group making a play. Someone who asked the right question, offered a new perspective, or listened with an empathetic ear. It's what happens when you put great players in the right environment. Magic happens and makes peer advantage possible.

WHAT PEER ADVANTAGE FEELS LIKE

There's something visceral about game day, or, as we call it, the day of the group meeting. Let's imagine an 8:00 a.m. arrival, as group members are filing in to the meeting location. They grab some hot coffee and a light breakfast. They catch up with one another casually on what's been happening in their companies and in their lives since the last meeting. Even if the group meets once a month, a lot can happen. During the previous month, you may have taken a vacation, acquired a new client, celebrated a birthday, or received a clean bill of health at your physical. Conversely, you may have worked nonstop, mourned the death of a loved one, lost a major customer, or learned that you or a family member requires surgery. The meetings are not simply about your company; they are about your life and the lives of those you care about, both inside and outside the group.

The individual conversations fade as people take their seats and the meeting gets started. Often, a leader kicks off the meeting by having everyone take a turn to report on how he feels personally and professionally, and to talk about any company developments since the last meeting. This check-in not only keeps everyone apprised of what's going on with everyone else, but also serves to identify issues or opportunities these CEOs may want to bring to the group for deeper discussion. It also sets the tone for the kind of conversations that will likely take place during the day, particularly when someone shares difficult news or something that's deeply personal during the check-in.

Within the first twenty minutes, it's clear this not an ordinary gathering. It is an entirely different kind of engagement. It requires a level of involvement, candor, and accountability that is missing from the business meetings most of us attend each day.

Some CEO groups invite speakers that the group leader believes will offer relevant and educational takeaways. Other groups meet for a specified period of time, possibly a full or half day, and after the group members check in with one another, they'll start formally processing issues or opportunities, or, as Etienne Wenger-Trayner likes to call them, case clinics. In chapter 7, we walked you through the issue processing flow chart that is commonly used to analyze and work cases in real time.

We've covered the mechanics of the process, but Mike Richardson describes what it feels like to be in the room and work an issue with a group:

> At the very beginning of the meeting, you notice that you're already past the garden-variety peer influence end of the

Issue / Opportunity Flowchart

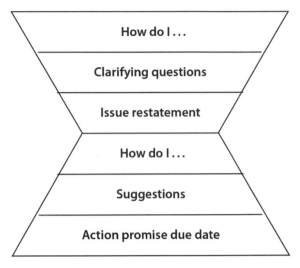

How do I ...

Clarifying questions

Issue restatement

How do I ...

Suggestions

Action promise due date

FIGURE 11.2　Issue Processing Protocol

spectrum. Things quickly crystallize though, and as they start to gel, we progress to the advantage end of the spectrum. You can feel it. You can taste it. You can see it. You can feel that different context, that different aura, the different gravity. It can start as early as the pregame stuff that's going on as people are connecting before the meeting formally begins.

Obviously, I think the differentiating moment between influence and advantage happens when you're in the middle of discussing a complex issue, or what I like to call a *wheelspin* issue. It's so tangled that this member may well have been spinning their wheels on it for quite some time, and here we are in the middle of it and there's just something very powerful that it may not sound like it or look like it or even feel like it to an outsider, but to an insider, you know there's something very special happening. It's quiet when it needs to be, it's noisy when it needs to be; we are in the moment, we are very present, we are listening and looking, and you can feel the epiphany is coming and you can see, hear, and feel things shift.

It may not be a singular earth-shattering comment or question or idea from anybody. It's not always sharp, it's often blunt. It can be just the compounding effect of the member who's being listened to for thirty-five, forty-five, sixty, ninety minutes, and being appreciated and cared for. After the member has taken a moment to reflect, we say, "What have you heard and what's resonating with you?" They'll say something like, "You guys have left such a footprint and impact upon me, I can't tell you how big an impact all of this is."

Lightbulbs come on in my head in some way, shape, or form, and I think it's that depth, it's that height of shift—and it takes time to get there, although it happens a lot faster than you might think. I think that's the advantage. You can't buy that. You can't get that. You have to invest in that and then, you belong to it. You've earned the right to be part of it and it shows up.

The passion and energy of Mike's words are palpable. This is just one example of what makes the peer advantage experience so powerful. In essence, there are few, if any, forums in which CEOs can sit down with a group of people and be totally honest and vulnerable without having their guard up. The CEOs who want to avail themselves of that kind of forum trust one another enough to create it. With each passing meeting, there's a little bit of extra trust, an increased willingness to be open—and the more people do this, the more trust builds in the group. It creates the necessary atmosphere of emotional and intellectual safety so necessary for this kind of experience.

Larry Hart, who leads CEO peer groups in Atlanta, describes trust and how it develops in a group this way:

When I think about what makes a CEO group tick, it's all about trust. Absolute trust. It's how you develop that trust that is unique to the group experience, and while it happens faster than you might imagine, it doesn't happen overnight. It happens when you sit in that room time and time again, and it's reinforced each time you spend time together outside of the group meeting. Maybe you go on a retreat, and you act goofy for a couple of nights or something along those lines. People share stories from the retreats over and over again and they become part of the lexicon. They develop a trust.

Larry shared a book with us called *The Third Opinion* by Saj-nicole A. Joni. She talked about trust as falling into three buckets, and Larry has used this model successfully for years now in leading four peer groups—two for CEOs and two for key executives. The buckets are as follows: (1) We trust people personally because we get to know who they are as a person. We trust friends and colleagues whom we get to know socially. (2) We trust people for their subject-matter expertise. We trust a pilot we've never met to fly us across the country or a surgeon to perform an operation. (3) We trust people to have our backs, to not have a personal agenda and use something against us. This is structural trust. For a CEO peer group, it's easy to see how the triad provides the necessary structure for building trust on all three levels.

When you look at a roomful of CEOs come together, they're ultimately creating a comfortable and productive space for one another—there's a sense of people getting to know one another, of these people running businesses—and they learn to trust their group members' advice. And while the CEOs care about every member's success, they have no hidden agendas or a stake in the outcome that would adversely influence them in any way.

THE JOURNEY FROM PEER INFLUENCE TO PEER ADVANTAGE

Our purpose in writing this book was to introduce you to an option for learning and growing personally and professionally that you may not be accessing as a CEO. It may be because you didn't know the option was available, you believe you don't have enough time to participate, or you're not sure what group to join or how to start your own; or perhaps it's because, once you've learned about peer groups, you came to the conclusion that they're not right for you. You're in the majority. Fewer than 1 percent of CEOs participate in CEO peer advisory groups, yet most of the high-performing CEOs who are members of a group say their experience has lifted their organizations and changed their lives beyond measure. Because this feels like such a disconnect, we thought that we would provide a closer look at what it's all about for the remaining 99 percent, and we hope that you'll give it a try.

The journey began with a look at the pervasive nature of peer influence. It's been a part of our lives for as long as we can remember, and it impacts us in ways that are so buried in our subconscious we don't even recognize them. Next time you throw money in the guitar case of a street musician, ask yourself why you did it. It's likely that you just followed the lead of another generous soul who also enjoys good music.

For CEOs, tapping into peer influence can matter a great deal for two important reasons. Now that you've ascended to the position of CEO, the number of people around you who know precisely what it's like to sit in that chair and make decisions on behalf of an entire company are few and far between. There are certain challenges and topics that you just can't raise with your employees or even your board of directors. You can read books filled with case studies of how CEOs handled similar situations, but who can you rely on to help you with what keeps you up at night? A second reason is that, despite a strong organizational structure for getting things done, certain initiatives you undertake are unsuccessful. You likely had a good plan and smart people working on it, but they may not have had the kind of influence to inspire their peers to row the boat in the same direction with perfect synchronicity. Understanding the dynamics that run horizontally in your organization is every bit as important as understanding those that run vertically. Employees influence other employees enormously. You can either tap into that peer influence or be the victim of it.

Because peer influence affects everyone, including CEOs and organizational leaders of all kinds, it can be helpful to understand how people typically engage their peers and for what purpose. Our peer engagement framework illustrates what peer engagement looks like. We connect, network, optimize, and accelerate.

We **connect** with our peers in person or online. We connect to review, to gather and exchange information and to extend our reach both personally and professionally. We're not necessarily selective about our peers when we connect, but we tend to trust the prevailing sentiment of the community even more than private or government institutions.

We **network** online and at conferences, or at local business events and socials. Here we tend to be more selective and more purposeful in our attempt to advance personal and professional interests. Connecting and networking are individual activities, and are the most common ways we reach out to our peers.

We **optimize** when we work together in teams to bring a high level of excellence toward achieving a common goal. We discussed a number of nonbusiness examples to paint the picture of what optimizing looks like, but organizational leaders often assemble tiger teams, small teams of people who are brought together to tackle special projects or improve performance. The work of optimizing tends to take place among a more homogenous group of peers, and is more temporary in nature, determined by either the length of a project or the span of a season.

CEOs **accelerate** their business and leadership growth when they are members of peer advisory groups and work together on an ongoing basis. Their groups embody the five factors for gaining peer advantage. Their objectives are to help one another meet tough challenges, achieve lofty organizational goals, and grow as leaders.

We purposely covered these concepts in the order in which they are most frequently accessed. Generally speaking, people tend to connect more than network, network more than optimize, and optimize more

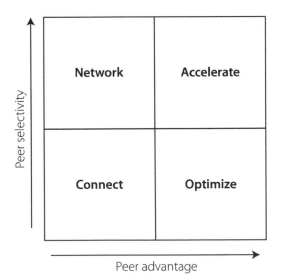

FIGURE 11.3   Peer Engagement Framework

than accelerate. Because CEOs' and business leaders' time is extremely valuable, we recommend investing energy in these peer engagement activities in the opposite order presented—for CEOs, the greatest return on investment happens when they accelerate.

Let's take one more look at the five essential factors necessary for creating the conditions for realizing peer advantage.

Select the right peers. This involves more than surrounding yourself with the right people. Based on your personal and professional goals, selecting the right peers requires that you reflect on whether you are well suited for a group experience, and that you understand how to evaluate whether a group is right for you and how you know if your group is providing you with true peer advantage.

Create a safe environment. Deep conversations about critical intellectual and emotional issues require an environment in which it is safe to share and be vulnerable (judgment free), and where confidentiality is sacrosanct. What happens in the meeting stays in the meeting.

Utilize a smart guide. Whether a group is led by a member or a professional facilitator, maximizing the potential of any group depends on skilled leadership. We tapped the experience of some of the world's best CEO peer advisory group leaders to learn more about how they lead their groups for optimal peer advantage. They do so by acting as a guide and considering themselves an equal part of the peer advisory group triad.

Foster valuable interaction. A group culture that values safety and confidentiality is an important first step, but conversations that help members achieve their goals and processes don't happen by accident—they happen by design. Rich dialogue can lead to positive outcomes and serve as the intellectual counterbalance to the emotional safety provided by the group.

Be accountable. If you're a member of a group that optimizes and accelerates well, the group members don't tell you what you should do; you tell them what you plan to do. Once you do that, you not only own the solution, your fellow members will expect you to do what you say you will do (DWYSYWD). This level of group accountability gives peer advantage its punctuation.

If you are surrounded by good people who work as a triad and practice the fundamentals of the five factors, the rest is up to you. The people of the group make the group—they are the ones who make the plays that make a difference.

While we may have waited until chapter 9 to write about it, organizational growth and business success start with individual growth. For CEOs who come to their groups to listen and learn, it's a growth experience like no other. Most members won't simply talk about how they are better CEOs for having been involved in their groups, they'll talk about how they have grown as leaders, friends, spouses, and community members.

Additionally, it's incumbent upon the CEO to ask the "What if?" questions. Unless you carve out the time to step outside your company and industry to meet with others and contemplate a world of uncertainty, it's unlikely to ever happen. The world is changing faster than most of us can imagine. Between 1950 and 2020, the world population is expected to have tripled. This staggering population growth will be accompanied by unimaginable changes in the years and decades to come.

Our purpose for writing this book was to open up your minds to what we know is one of the most powerful, proven, and efficient leadership tools for enhancing the value of your business and your life. A diverse group of your peers will help you identify your blind spots, challenge your assumptions, and provide you with the kind of insights you'll need to succeed and thrive. Joining a peer group is as critical to your success as having the right team running your business. There's no need to go it alone. Roughly two-thirds of CEOs don't get the benefit of outside leadership advice or objective guidance from outside of their industry. You don't have to be one of them.

Simply put, peer advantage is power. Power to change, power to manifest your vision, power to win, and power to differentiate you from your competitors. And perhaps the biggest win, the greatest gift peer advantage will give you, is freedom. Freedom to live and love your life as you choose. Enjoy the journey. We can't wait to find out where it takes you.

I am
because
you are.
—African proverb

AFTERWORD

by Sam Reese, Chief Executive Officer,
Vistage Worldwide, Inc.

Like so many things with leadership, it all starts at the top—and embracing peer advantage for your organization is no different. As a veteran member of Vistage, one who credits much of my professional success to the peers who joined me for my journey in building Miller Heiman into one of the largest sales-effectiveness companies in the world, I know the tangible benefit peer advantage can play in an organization.

The Annual Client Summit we held at Miller Heiman is a classic example. In 2000, only a small handful of clients attended our first event. By 2014 there were several hundred attendees, and they created world-class presentations, sharing their success stories and best practices in the spirit of generosity and collaboration. Our clients encouraged one another to raise the bar in every way imaginable through the sheer power of their example. Each new summit eclipsed the previous year's, as the event grew in numbers and in quality. We simply provided the setting that enabled clients to work together. We communicated our new research and announced new products, and our clients learned from one another in myriad ways. Peer advantage was firing on all cylinders.

Fortunately, these learnings translated into success for the business I ran for fifteen years. Our people not only cared about results, they cared about one another and the clients we served (which, as you know, is what real success looks like). And now, several years later, my ever-evolving relationship with peer advantage has thankfully led me to the CEO role at Vistage. Utilizing mentors and trusted advisors has long been key to the success of many executives. Access to the insights and experience of people who have already navigated the complex waters of effective leadership is invaluable. There is little debate about the benefits of mentorship and peer advice. The key is to operationalize this support so that executives can get access to the answers they need at the time they need it. So ask yourself not only who you are turning to, but who key members of your management team are turning to. I challenge CEOs of all shapes and sizes to harness this power for their enterprises.

Despite unprecedented advances in technology and the seemingly countless ways we can connect and communicate across continents, the value of face-to-face communication with our peers has never been more relevant. As the world becomes increasingly complex, the next generation of leaders will need one another more than ever. If we can succeed in cultivating peer advantage with today's natural networkers, there's no limit to what we can accomplish in the years ahead—and there's no limit to the myriad benefits not only to a business's bottom line but, more importantly, to the lives of those involved.

With this in mind, I can't think of a more exciting and purposeful opportunity. With a little help from my group members, I look forward to bringing peer advantage into the lives of organizational leaders on every corner of the globe for years to come.

ACKNOWLEDGMENTS

As you would imagine, writing a book about peer advantage and the power of peers is not something one should attempt alone. To capture the nuances and benefits of peer advantage, we benefited from reading some outstanding research studies and drew upon the wisdom of dozens of CEOs, business owners, scholars, organizational leaders, authors, peer advisory group leaders, and competitors alike. We are grateful to everyone who embraced this mission and participated, either actively or passively, in helping us put the power of peers into words.

We'd first like to acknowledge our Vistage community, including the board of directors, leadership team, staff, chairs, members, and speakers both here in the U.S. and around the world. Because of their knowledge and experience, we asked better questions and received keener insights from all the people we interviewed. The members of our respective Vistage peer advisory groups have been listening to us talk about this book for more than a year; we appreciate their support and their participation in this endeavor. Vistage Chief Marketing Officer Kathleen Delaney was particularly helpful in keeping us focused and providing the strategic direction and editorial support we needed to bring peer advantage to life.

Rich Karlgaard, who has written a number of books, most recently *Team Genius* and *The Soft Edge*, not only offered early encouragement, but also generously agreed to write the Foreword. Sam Reese, former CEO of Miller Heiman, Vistage member, and now CEO of Vistage Worldwide immediately embraced the idea of writing about peer advantage from a broader perspective rather than from a singularly Vistage point of view. Sam's Afterword demonstrates his firsthand knowledge and commitment to the power of peer advisory groups and their infinite possibilities for the future.

We're deeply appreciative of Heather Pemberton Levy who served as our editor and "chief everything officer." Her guidance and ongoing support over the past year, from how the book should be organized to the best way to tell a meaningful and relevant story, proved invaluable to this effort. Heather was also kind enough to introduce us to our publisher, Bibliomotion, Inc., and its talented team who provided the perfect blend of advice and support we needed as first-time authors. We also extend our thanks to KemperLesnik Public Relations, who will undoubtedly extend the reach of peer advantage well beyond the pages of this book.

We owe a debt of gratitude to those who contributed to the content and provided editorial and other critical support services, without whom there would be no book. Thanks to Dean Acosta, Brandon Andrews, Angel Aristone, Doug Baker, Bob Berk, Fredricka Brecht, Stephanie Breneman, Chris Brogan, Dan Bucko, Julie Burger, Alejo Canton, Greg Bustin, Reid Carr, Richard Carr, Paul Caskey, Fred Chaney, Sherine Cheng, Richard Curtin, Bob Dabic, Scot Dietz, Rick Dool, Bob Duncan, Steve Dobbins, Janet Fogarty, Steve Gilroy, Laura Goodrich, Shannon Gray, Don Guild, Linda Gabbard, Ozzie Gontang, Verne Harnish, Larry Hart, Larry Hawks, Hazel Henderson, Sue Hesse, Jeannette Hobson, Mary Hoffman, Leigh Hooker, Patrick Houlahan, Laura Hughes, Danielle Itani, Saundra Johnson, John Kenney, Nick King, Mike Klowden, Jim Kouzes, Jean Lauterbach, Geoff Lawrence, Christopher Lee, Marissa Levin, Charlene Li, Todd Lingle, Dave Logan, Martin Lynch, Ken McLeod, Cheryl McMillan, Katie McWeeney, Declan Maguire, Nanda Mbengue, Michael Molina, Zachary Morowitz, Nicole Mouskondis, Mark Murphy, Chris Noonan, Martha Oxley, Rafael Pastor, Bob Pittman, Shea Ralph, Mike Richardson, JJ Ramberg, Norma Rosenberg, Paul Sabattus, Pete Sciabarra, Carol Sharicz, Jan Sias, Frank Silverstein, Brian Solis, Robin Stanaland, Jay Steinfeld, Diane Stewart, Nigel Stoke, Lynn Tanner, Teigue Thomas, Robert H. Thompson, Ashley Timms, Dejah Urbanovitch, Patty Vogan, Megan Webb-Morgan, Beverly Wenger-Trayner, Etienne Wenger-Trayner,

Richard Wong, Cecelia Wooden, Kaleigh Woodhart, Morgan Xu, and David Zerfoss.

All of the amazing support we received to write this book, and for whatever we may have achieved in life, is a testament to the power of peers. None of us does it alone. There's another type of support we received that only comes from family. Leon's wife Debra and Leo's wife Ellyne provided invaluable editorial and emotional support, and Leon's daughter Danielle and son Adam, and Leo's daughters Kristin and Taylor, who are all leaders in their own right, offered their perspectives on the next generation, and they continue to teach us something new every day.

NOTES

Introduction

1. David F. Larcker, Stephen Miles, Brian Tayan, and Michelle E. Gutman, "2013 Executive Coaching Survey," Stanford Graduate School of Business, August 1, 2013, accessed November 3, 2015, https://www.gsb.stanford.edu/faculty-research /publications/2013-executive-coaching-survey.

Chapter 1

1. David F. Larcker, Stephen Miles, Brian Tayan, and Michelle E. Gutman, "2013 Executive Coaching Survey," Stanford Graduate School of Business, August 1, 2013, accessed November 3, 2015, https://www.gsb.stanford.edu/faculty-research /publications/2013-executive-coaching-survey.
2. Richard Branson, "Richard Branson on Not Going It Alone," *Entrepreneur,* February 17, 2014, accessed September 26, 2015, http://www.entrepreneur.com /article/231523.
3. Jean Lave and Etienne Wenger, *Situated Learning: Legitimate Peripheral Participation* (Cambridge, England: Cambridge University Press, 1991).
4. Etienne Wenger and Richard A. McDermott, *Cultivating Communities of Practice: A Guide to Managing Knowledge* (Boston, MA: Harvard Business School Press, 2002), 4.
5. Etienne C. Wenger and William M. Snyder, "Communities of Practice: The Organizational Frontier," *Harvard Business Review,* January–February 2000.
6. "Citizen Ben," PBS, accessed September 1, 2015, http://www.pbs.org/benfranklin /l3_citizen_networker.html.
7. "Citizen Ben."
8. Napoleon Hill, *Think and Grow Rich: Original* 1937 edition (Duke Classics, 2012).
9. "The 2015 Millennial Majority Workforce: Study Results," commissioned by Elance–oDesk and Millennial Branding, October 2014, accessed September 16, 2015, http://www.slideshare.net/oDesk/2015-millennial-majority-workforce.
10. "The 2015 Millennial Majority Workforce: Study Results."

Chapter 2

1. Jeff Banowetz, "Bruce Cleland: The First Charity Runner," Competitor.com, January 31, 2013, accessed September 1, 2015, http://running.competitor.com/2013/01/features/bruce-cleland-the-first-charity-runner_65166.

2. Banowetz, "Bruce Cleland."

3. "Children's Peer Relationships Have Enormous Influence," EurekAlert!, accessed September 6, 2015, http://www.eurekalert.org/pub_releases/2006-01/asu-cpr 012406.php.

4. Albert Bandura, *Self-Efficacy: The Exercise of Control* (New York: W. H. Freeman and Company, 1997).

5. Melissa Kelly, "Cooperative Learning Versus Traditional Learning in Groups," About.com, accessed September 6, 2015, http://712educators.about.com/od/cooplearning/tp/Cooperative-Learning-Versus-Traditional-Learning-For-Group-Activities.htm.

6. Mark L. Knapp, *Handbook of Interpersonal Communication*, 3rd ed. (Beverly Hills, CA: Sage Publications, 2002), 618.

7. Knapp, *Handbook of Interpersonal Communication*.

8. Stephen M. R. Covey and Rebecca R. Merrill, *The Speed of Trust: The One Thing That Changes Everything* (New York: Free Press, 2006).

9. Ken Blanchard, "Managing the Art of Change." Trainingjournal.com, 2010, 44–47.

10. "2015 Edelman Trust Barometer: Executive Summary," Edelman, 2015, accessed September 30, 2015, http://www.scribd.com/doc/252750985/2015-Edelman-Trust-Barometer-Executive-Summary.

11. "About Net Promoter," Bain & Company, accessed September 30, 2015, http://netpromotersystem.com/about/index.aspx.

12. Frederick F. Reichheld and Rob Markey, *The Ultimate Question 2.0: How Net Promoter Companies Thrive in a Customer-Driven World*, rev. ed. (Boston: Harvard Business Press, 2011).

13. Kelton Rhoads, "Get-A-Mac Campaign Analysis," *Working Psychology*, January 10, 2007, http://www.workingpsychology.com/download_folder/GAM_Campaign_Analysis.pdf.

14. Vladas Griskevicius, Robert B. Cialdini, and Noah J. Goldstein, "Applying (and Resisting) Peer Influence," *MIT Sloan Management Review*, Winter 2008.

15. Edward T. Hall, *Beyond Culture* (Garden City, NY: Anchor Press, 1976).

16. "TIME Magazine's Person of the Year," *Information Today*, February 1, 200.

17. C. M. K. Cheung, M. K. O. Lee, and Z. W. Y. Lee, "Understanding the Continuance Intention of Knowledge Sharing in Online Communities of Practice Through the Post-Knowledge-Sharing Evaluation Processes," *J. Am. Soc. Inf. Sci*, 2013.

18. Nate Silver, "The Huskies Are Better Than the Wildcats Ever Hoped to Be," *FiveThirtyEight* blog, April 6, 2015, accessed September 1, 2015.

Chapter 3

1. Richard Feloni, "How Jimmy Fallon Made It to 'The Tonight Show' Through Exceptional Networking," *Business Insider*, November 6, 2014, accessed September 5, 2015, http://www.businessinsider.com/jimmy-fallon-networking-key-to-success -2014-11.
2. Deborah Stoll, "How a Million-Dollar Toy Changed Networking in YPO," Young Presidents Organization YPO, December 7, 2014, accessed September 25, 2015, http://www.ypo.org/2014/12/how-a-million-dollar-toy-changed-networ king-in-ypo/.
3. Stoll, "How a Million-Dollar Toy Changed Networking in YPO."
4. "Canadian Networking and Its Impact on Careers, Business and Economy: A Survey of Networking Practices, Systems and Opinions," 2009, accessed November 17, 2015, http://www.connectuscanada.com/ebooks/canadian-networking -survey.pdf.
5. Simon Sinek, "A Special Webinar with Simon Sinek: Innovate or Get Left Behind," *Fridays with Vistage*, September 21, 2012.
6. Peter M. Senge, *The Fifth Discipline· The Art and Practice of the Learning Organization* (New York: Doubleday/Currency, 1990), 3.
7. James M. Kouzes and Barry Z. Posner, *The Leadership Challenge*, 3rd ed. (San Francisco: Jossey-Bass, 2002).

Chapter 4

1. David Logan and John Paul King, *Tribal Leadership: Leveraging Natural Groups to Build a Thriving Organization* (New York: Collins, 2008).
2. Logan and King, *Tribal Leadership*.
3. Marshall Goldsmith, "Try Feedforward Instead of Feedback," Marshall Goldsmith Library, accessed September 5, 2015, http://www.marshallgoldsmith library.com/cim/articles_display.php?aid=110.
4. Jim Alampi, *Great to Excellent; It's the Execution!* (CreateSpace Independent Publishing Platform, 2013).

Chapter 5

1. Brené Brown, *Daring Greatly: How the Courage to Be Vulnerable Transforms the Way We Live, Love, Parent, and Lead* (New York: Gotham Books, 2012).
2. Hesse Partners, Sample Forum Norms, accessed September 5, 2015, http:// www.hessepartners.com/assets/Forum-Norms-SAMPLE-Hesse-Partners .pdf, 1.
3. Hesse Partners, Sample Forum Norms, 2–3.
4. Brené Brown, "The Power of Vulnerability," TED Talk, June 2010, accessed September 5, 2015, http://www.ted.com/talks/brene_brown_on_vulnerability ?language=en.

Chapter 6

1. Ken M. Keith, interview, "Servant Leadership in Dr. Keith's Own Words," *Client Services Insight (CSI)* blog, April 30, 2008, accessed September 17, 2015, http://clientserviceinsights.blogspot.com/2008/04/servant-leadership-in-dr-keiths-own.html.
2. Stanley Deetz, Sarah J. Tracy, and Jennifer Lyn Simpson, *Leading Organizations Through Transition: Communication and Cultural Change* (Thousand Oaks, CA: Sage Publications, 2000).
3. Keith, "Servant Leadership in Dr. Keith's Own Words."
4. Bill George and Doug Baker, *True North Groups: A Powerful Path to Personal and Leadership Development* (San Francisco: Berrett-Koehler Publishers, 2011).

Chapter 7

1. Robert J. Garmston and Bruce M. Wellman, *Educational Leadership* 55, no. 7 (1998): 30.
2. John Foley. "Glad to Be Here: Lessons in High Performance from the Blue Angels," *Leader to Leader*, 2013, 42.
3. Sid Heal, "Debriefings and After Action Reviews," *The Tactical Edge*, 2009, accessed November 10, 2015, http://www.justiceacademy.org/iShare/Heal/Debriefings and After Action Reviews.pdf.
4. Katie McKinney Maddalena, ""I Need You to Say 'I' ": Why First Person Is Important in College Writing," 2010, accessed November 10, 2015, http://www.parlorpress.com/pdf/mckinney-maddalena--i-need-you-to-say-i.pdf.

Chapter 8

1. Pasi Sahlberg and Andy Hargreaves, *Finnish Lessons: What Can the World Learn from Educational Change in Finland?* (New York: Teachers College Press, 2011).
2. Anu Partanen, "What Americans Keep Ignoring About Finland's School Success," *Atlantic*, December 29, 2011.
3. "Psychology of Procrastination: Why People Put Off Important Tasks Until the Last Minute, American Psychological Association, April 5, 2010, accessed November 10, 2015, http://www.apa.org/news/press/releases/2010/04/procrastination.aspx.
4. Bruce W. Tuckman, Dennis A. Abry, and Dennis R. Smith, *Learning and Motivation Strategies: Your Guide to Success*, 2nd ed. (Upper Saddle River, NJ: Pearson/Prentice Hall, 2008), 17.
5. Cheryl McMillan, "What Makes a Person Accountable, Part 2—Vistage Executive Street Blog." Vistage Executive Street Blog. January 10, 2012. Accessed December 19, 2015. http://blog.vistage.com/business-strategy-and-management/what-makes-a-person-accountable-part-2/.

6. Greg Bustin, *Accountability: The Key to Driving a High-Performance Culture* (New York: McGraw Hill Education, 2014).

Chapter 9

1. B. Candace Beeke, "Blinds.com Founder Jay Steinfeld's Journey from Soda Fountain Jerk to Entrepreneur," *Houston Business Journal*, January 31, 2014, accessed September 23, 2015, http://www.bizjournals.com/houston/print-edition/2014/01/31/an-unexpected-journey-an-entrepreneurs-dream-come.html.
2. Peter M. Senge, *The Fifth Discipline: The Art and Practice of the Learning Organization* (New York: Doubleday/Currency, 1990).
3. Marshall Goldsmith and Mark Reiter, *What Got You Here Won't Get You There: How Successful People Become Even More Successful* (New York: Hyperion, 2007).

Chapter 10

1. Peter M. Senge, *The Fifth Discipline: The Art and Practice of the Learning Organization* (New York: Doubleday/Currency, 1990), 361.
2. G. James Lemoine and Nathan Bennett, "What VUCA Really Means for You, *Harvard Business Review*, January–February 2014.
3. "No Battle Plan Survives Contact with the Enemy," *Lexician*, accessed September 17, 2015, http://www.lexician.com/lexblog/2010/11/no-battle-plan-survives-contact-with-the-enemy/.
4. Lisamarie Babik, "Plans Are Useless, but Planning Is Indispensable," 2005, accessed November 10, 2015, http://www.menloinnovations.com/by-reading/PDF/Plans.pdf.
5. Lemoine and Bennett, "What VUCA Really Means for You."
6. "No Battle Plan Survives Contact with the Enemy," *Lexician*.
7. Angela Wilkinson and Roland Kupers, "Living in the Futures," *Harvard Business Review*, May 1, 2013, accessed September 7, 2015.
8. "Scenario and Contingency Planning," Bain & Company, June 10, 2015, accessed September 7, 2015, http://www.bain.com/publications/articles/management-tools-scenario-and-contingency-planning.aspx.

REFERENCES

Alampi, Jim. *Great to Excellent; It's the Execution!* CreateSpace Independent Publishing Platform, 2013.

American Psychological Association. "Psychology of Procrastination: Why People Put Off Important Tasks Until the Last Minute." American Psychological Association, April 5, 2010. Accessed November 10, 2015. http://www.apa.org/news/press/releases/2010/04/procrastination.aspx.

Arizona State University. "Children's Peer Relationships Have Enormous Influence." EurekAlert! Accessed September 6, 2015. http://www.eurekalert.org/pub_releases/2006-01/asu-cpr012406.php.

Babik, Lisamarie. "Plans Are Useless, but Planning Is Indispensable." PMI Global Congress Procceedings, 2005. Accessed November 10, 2015. http://www.menloinnovations.com/by-reading/PDF/Plans.pdf.

Bain & Company. "About Net Promoter." Accessed September 30, 2015. http://netpromotersystem.com/about/index.aspx.

Bain & Company. "Scenario and Contingency Planning." Bain & Company, June 10, 2015. Accessed September 7, 2015. http://www.bain.com/publications/articles/management-tools-scenario-and-contingency-planning.aspx.

Bandura, Albert. *Self-Efficacy: The Exercise of Control.* New York: W. H. Freeman and Company, 1997.

Banowetz, Jeff. "Bruce Cleland: The First Charity Runner." Competitor.com, January 31, 2013. Accessed September 1, 2015. http://running.competitor.com/2013/01/features/bruce-cleland-the-first-charity-runner_65166.

Beeke, B. Candace. "Blinds.com Founder Jay Steinfeld's Journey from Soda Fountain Jerk to Entrepreneur." *Houston Business Journal*, January 31, 2014. Accessed September 23, 2015. http://www.bizjournals.com/houston/print-edition/2014/01/31/an-unexpected-journey-an-entrepreneurs-dream-come.html.

Blanchard, Ken. "Managing the Art of Change." *Training Journal*, 2010.

Branson, Richard. "Richard Branson on Not Going It Alone." *Entrepreneur*, February 17, 2014. Accessed September 26, 2015. http://www.entrepreneur.com/article/231523.

Brown, Brené. *Daring Greatly: How the Courage to Be Vulnerable Transforms the Way We Live, Love, Parent, and Lead*. New York: Gotham Books, 2012.

Brown, Brené. "The Power of Vulnerability." TED Talk, June 2010. Accessed September 5, 2015. http://www.ted.com/talks/brene_brown_on_vulnerability?language=en.

Bustin, Greg. *Accountability: The Key to Driving a High-Performance Culture*. New York: McGraw Hill Education, 2014.

Cheung, C. M. K., M. K. O. Lee, and Z. W. Y. Lee. "Understanding the Continuance Intention of Knowledge Sharing in Online Communities of Practice Through the Post-Knowledge-Sharing Evaluation Processes." *Journal of the American Society of Information Science and Technology*, 2013.

Connect Us Communications Canada and PeopleCoach. *Canadian Networking and Its Impact on Careers, Business, and Economy: A Survey of Networking Practices, Systems, and Opinions*. Connect Us Communications Canada and PeopleCoach, 2009. Accessed November 17, 2015. http://www.connectuscanada.com/ebooks/canadian-networking-survey.pdf.

Covey, Stephen M. R., and Rebecca R. Merrill. *The Speed of Trust: The One Thing That Changes Everything*. New York: Free Press, 2006.

Deetz, Stanley, Sarah J. Tracy, and Jennifer Lyn Simpson. *Leading Organizations Through Transition: Communication and Cultural Change*. Thousand Oaks, CA: Sage Publications, 2000.

Edelman. "2015 Edelman Trust Barometer: Executive Summary." Accessed September 30, 2015. http://www.scribd.com/doc/252750985/2015-Edelman-Trust-Barometer-Executive-Summary.

Elance-oDesk and Millennial Branding. "The 2015 Millennial Majority Workforce: Study Results." *2015 Millennial Majority Workforce: Study Results*. Accessed September 16, 2015. http://www.slideshare.net/oDesk/2015-millennial-majority-workforce.

Feloni, Richard. "How Jimmy Fallon Made It to 'The Tonight Show' Through Exceptional Networking." *Business Insider*, November 6, 2014. Accessed September 5, 2015. http://www.businessinsider.com/jimmy-fallon-networking-key-to-success-2014-11.

Foley, John. "Glad to Be Here: Lessons in High Performance from the Blue Angels." *Leader to Leader* 2013, no. 67 (2013): 36–42.

Garmston, Robert J., and Bruce M. Wellman. *Educational Leadership* 55, no. 7 (1998).

George, Bill, and Doug Baker. *True North Groups: A Powerful Path to Personal and Leadership Development*. San Francisco: Berrett-Koehler Publishers, 2011.

Goldsmith, Marshall. "Try Feedforward Instead of Feedback." Marshall Goldsmith Library, adapted from *Leader to Leader*, Summer 2002. Accessed September 5, 2015. http://www.marshallgoldsmithlibrary.com/cim/articles_display.php?aid=110.

Goldsmith, Marshall, and Mark Reiter. *What Got You Here Won't Get You There: How Successful People Become Even More Successful*. New York: Hyperion, 2007.

Griskevicius, Vladas, Robert B. Cialdini, and Noah J. Goldstein. "Applying (and Resisting) Peer Influence." *MIT Sloan Management Review*, Winter 2008.

Hall, Edward T. *Beyond Culture*. Garden City, NY: Anchor Press, 1976.

Heal, Sid. "Debriefings and After Action Reviews." *Tactical Edge*, 2009. Accessed November 10, 2015. http://www.justiceacademy.org/iShare/Heal/Debriefings and After Action Reviews.pdf.

Hesse Partners. "Sample Forum Norms." Accessed September 5, 2015. http://www.hessepartners.com/assets/Forum-Norms-SAMPLE-Hesse-Partners.pdf.

Hill, Napoleon. *Think and Grow Rich: The Original Unedited 1937 Edition*. Duke Classics, 2012.

Keith, Kent M., "Servant Leadership in Dr. Keith's Own Words," *Client Services Insight (CSI)* blog, April 30, 2008. Accessed September 17, 2015. http://clientserviceinsights.blogspot.com/2008/04/servant-leadership-in-dr-keiths-own.html.

Kelly, Melissa. "Cooperative Learning Versus Traditional Learning in Groups." About.com. Accessed September 6, 2015. http://712educators.about.com/od/cooplearning/tp/Cooperative-Learning-Versus-Traditional-Learning-For-Group-Activities.htm.

Knapp, Mark L. *Handbook of Interpersonal Communication*. 3rd ed. Beverly Hills: Sage Publications, 2002.

Kouzes, James M., and Barry Z. Posner. *The Leadership Challenge*. 3rd ed. San Francisco: Jossey-Bass, 2002.

Larcker, David F., Stephen Miles, Brian Tayan, and Michelle E. Gutman. "2013 Executive Coaching Survey." Stanford Graduate School of Business, August 1, 2013. Accessed November 3, 2015. https://www.gsb.stanford.edu/faculty-research/publications/2013-executive-coaching-survey.

Lave, Jean, and Etienne Wenger. *Situated Learning: Legitimate Peripheral Participation*. Cambridge, England: Cambridge University Press, 1991.

Lemoine, G. James, and Nathan Bennett. "What VUCA Really Means for You." *Harvard Business Review*, January–February 2014.

Lexician. "No Battle Plan Survives Contact with the Enemy," *Lexician*, November 1, 2010. Accessed September 17, 2015. http://www.lexician.com/lexblog/2010/11/no-battle-plan-survives-contact-with-the-enemy/.

Logan, David, and John Paul King. *Tribal Leadership: Leveraging Natural Groups to Build a Thriving Organization*. New York: Collins, 2008.

Maddalena, Katie McKinney. "I Need You to Say 'I'": Why First Person Is Important in College Writing," in *Writing Spaces: Readings on Writing*, Volume 1. Parlor Press, 2010. Accessed November 10, 2015. http://www.parlorpress.com/pdf/mckinney-maddalena--i-need-you-to-say-i.pdf.

McMillan, Cheryl. "What Makes a Person Accountable, Part 2—Vistage Executive Street Blog." Vistage Executive Street Blog. January 10, 2012. Accessed December 19, 2015. http://blog.vistage.com/business-strategy-and-management/what-makes-a-person-accountable-part-2/.

Partanen, Anu. "What Americans Keep Ignoring About Finland's School Success." *Atlantic*, December 29, 2011. Accessed September 6, 2015. http://www.theatlantic.com/national/archive/2011/12/what-americans-keep-ignoring-about-finlands-school-success/250564/.

Reichheld, Frederick F., and Rob Markey. *The Ultimate Question 2.0: How Net Promoter Companies Thrive in a Customer-Driven World.* Rev. ed. Boston: Harvard Business Press, 2011.

Rhoads, Kelton. "Get-A-Mac Campaign Analysis." *Working Psychology*, January 10, 2007. Accessed September 6, 2015. http://www.workingpsychology.com/download_folder/GAM_Campaign_Analysis.pdf.

Sahlberg, Pasi, and Andy Hargreaves. *Finnish Lessons: What Can the World Learn from Educational Change in Finland?* New York: Teachers College Press, 2011.

Senge, Peter M. *The Fifth Discipline: The Art and Practice of the Learning Organization.* New York: Doubleday/Currency, 1990.

Silver, Nate. "The Huskies Are Better Than the Wildcats Ever Hoped to Be." *FiveThirtyEight* blog, April 6, 2015. Accessed September 1, 2015.

Sinek, Simon. "A Special Webinar with Simon Sinek: Innovate or Get Left Behind." *Fridays with Vistage*, September 21, 2012.

Stoll, Deborah. "How a Million-Dollar Toy Changed Networking in YPO." Young Presidents Organization YPO, December 7, 2014. Accessed September 25, 2015. http://www.ypo.org/2014/12/how-a-million-dollar-toy-changed-networking-in-ypo/.

Tuckman, Bruce W., Dennis A. Abry, and Dennis R. Smith. *Learning and Motivation Strategies: Your Guide to Success.* 2nd ed. Upper Saddle River, NJ: Pearson/Prentice Hall, 2008.

Twin Cities Public Television, Inc. "Citizen Ben," 2002. Accessed September 1, 2015. http://www.pbs.org/benfranklin/l3_citizen_networker.html.

Wenger, Etienne, and Richard A. McDermott. *Cultivating Communities of Practice: A Guide to Managing Knowledge.* Boston: Harvard Business School Press, 2002.

Wenger, Etienne C., and William M. Snyder. "Communities of Practice: The Organizational Frontier." *Harvard Business Review*, January–February 2000.

Wilkinson, Angela, and Roland Kupers. "Living in the Futures." *Harvard Business Review*, May 1, 2013. Accessed September 7, 2015.

INDEX

ABOUT THE AUTHORS

Leon Shapiro served as the CEO of Vistage Worldwide (2013-2016), the world's leading peer advisory membership organization for CEOs, business owners, and their key executives. He is a member of the Vistage Board of Directors and also a Director at The Advisory Board Company (NASDAQ: ABCO).

Between 2007 and 2011, Leon served as senior vice president, Strategy and Operations, at Warner Music Group. From 2005 to 2006, he served as group president of The NPD Group, Inc., a global provider of consumer and retail information, where he led all of their entertainment and technology related businesses.

From 1989 to 2004, Leon served as president, Gartner Executive Programs for Gartner, Inc., the leading provider of research and analysis on the global information technology industry. Leon earned his bachelor's degree in economics and political science from the Hebrew University of Jerusalem in Israel.

Leo Bottary is vice president, Peer Advantage for Vistage Worldwide, where he directs a thought leadership initiative on the power of peer advantage for business leaders. Leo also serves as an adjunct professor for Seton Hall University's Master of Arts in Strategic Communication and Leadership program (MASCL), where he leads online learning teams. In April 2015, he was named adjunct teacher of the year for Seton Hall's College of Communication and the Arts.

Prior to joining in 2010, Leo enjoyed a twenty-five-year career counseling leaders in strategic communication. During that time, he served as a senior vice president (Corporate Practice) and director of Client Service for the U.S. at Hill & Knowlton. He also founded an award-winning public relations agency, which he sold in 2000.

Leo earned a BA from Jacksonville University, an MA in Strategic Communication and Leadership from Seton Hall University and is expected to receive his EdD from Northeastern University with a concentration in Organizational Leadership in 2016. Leo's dissertation focuses on the power of peer influence for CEOs.